THE WORKING SPECTRUM

A LIBRARY OF PRACTICAL SUBROUTINES AND PROGRAMS

DAVID LAWRENCE

Sunshine Books, London

PROGRAM NOTES

The programs in this book were printed out with a special interface built by L. E. Listings, 1 Leswin Road, London N16. Their help has been invaluable.

There are two points to note with the listings:

1) Inverse and graphics characters have only been underlined, in order to keep them readable.
2) The ↑ symbol is always represented by ^.

First published 1982 by:
Sunshine Books (An imprint of Scot Press Ltd.)
12 – 13 Little Newport Street,
London WC2R 3LD

ISBN 0 946408 00 9

Cover designed by James McDonald

Photograph of ZX Spectrum kindly supplied by Sinclair Research Ltd.

Typeset and printed in England by Commercial Colour Press, London E7.

CONTENTS

FOREWORD

I wrote this book to fill what seemed to me to be a huge hole. The hole is the absence of any single work aimed at fulfilling the new micro-owner's dream that his or her machine will not simply be a toy, nor even an educational introduction to the silicon age, but a powerful tool, taking over all kinds of tasks and opening up a variety of new possibilities. The majority of books either consist mostly of trivia or assume too great a desire — perhaps even a capacity — to experiment.

I wanted to write a book based upon a collection of solid, sophisticated programs in such areas as data storage, finance, calculation, graphics, household management and education. Discussion of programming techniques and general issues would spring out of the programs in much the same way, perhaps, as a magazine article associated with a program. I hope that you will find the book that has emerged useful not only as a way of learning new programming techniques but also as a package of useful programs, offering the prospect of a wide range of applications which might otherwise only have been available either to those prepared to buy cassettes or those capable of writing a substantial program for themselves.

The package falls roughl,/ into five groups of programs, which are listed below. I was very conscious of the danger of simply presenting an indigestible mass of programs. For that reason, as well as the fact that it suits the Spectrum anyway, all the programs have been written in modular form. Full instructions for testing each module before moving on to the next are given in the text.

A typical section of the book takes the following form:

Program Heading: e.g. Spectrum Filing Cabinet
There follows a general introduction to the section, stating the advantages and disadvantages of using the Spectrum for this kind of application. This is followed by one or more sections on the specific programming techniques used for this application. These might include techniques of searching, pointer arrays and storing data in dimensioned strings. Each module used in the program is then examined in detail.

The text alongside the modules comes in three sections: a) a brief discussion of the purpose of the module and any particular points of interest raised: b) a commentary on the lines themselves, identifying examples of particular techniques and pointing out the units into which the module naturally falls: c) suggestions are given for some simple tests you might like to perform to satisfy yourself that the module is at least not disastrously awry before entering the next module.

Do take the tests seriously — they can save a great deal of heartache later on.

Once the complete list of modules has been given there is a brief review of the main lessons that may have been learned in the course of entering the program.

One of the advantages of this approach is that the modules could then be used in other contexts once their function was understood, a possibility which is made more attractive by the Spectrum's ability to merge programs.

The ability of the Spectrum to accept several statements on a single Basic line can be a blessing or a curse. For ease of use and editing I have avoided using multi-statement lines when new applications are being tackled.

There are three ways then in which you can use this book:
1) As a novel way of learning how to program
2) As a package of useful applications programs
3) As a large collection of modules, or subroutines, which can be used in an unlimited number of other programs. You will find at the back of the book an extensive index covering the functions of each of the programming modules.

In other words you can treat this book as an introduction to more sophisticated programming, a library of useful programs or as a programming reference manual. To get the most out of the book, however, I recommend that you do start at the beginning and work your way through.

As a matter of learning technique you will find it useful to read the summary of the book below a couple of times, to give yourself a feel for the whole book. As you approach each section read the section introduction, skip through the section and read the summary. Then read the whole section. This way you will remember far more of the content.

CHAPTER 1

FINDING A FILE — The Spectrum as a filing cabinet

1.1 Unifile

Sooner or later most micro owners realize that their new digital friend comes into its own when it is storing information, processing it and presenting it in ways that would be laborious if done manually. They soon begin the task of writing simple programs which will store their friends' names and addresses or catalogue their stamp album. They may end up with half a dozen programs, all of them using roughly the same method but working on different types of information. In this chapter we examine how a single program can be written to cover a variety of filing tasks without the need for constant re-writing every time a new usage comes along.

Before we write the program we must decide on an economical way of storing the data we wish to file. Small programs can afford to fudge this issue since they are unlikely to make use of all the available memory anyway. Such a small program might, for instance, declare an array with dimensions of 50,4,20. This would allow the storage of up to 50 entries, each with four constituent items, each item being up to 20 characters long. The advantage of this is that each entry to the file would be clearly identifiable since entry X would be made up, if the array were called A$, of A$(X,1),A$(X,2),A$(X,3) and A$(X,4).

The disadvantage of this method is that for most filing uses it is likely to result in an enormous waste of space within the limited amount of memory available. The reason for this is simply that the length of the fixed space you allocate to each item must be adequate to the longest item you are likely to input. If, for instance, you want to store the names of your friends and one of them is graced with the surname Farquarson-Smythe, then you will have to set aside at least 17 characters for every surname, despite the fact that the rest of your friends are nowhere near so impressively named. The space allocated to most of the names would be more than half empty.

This is a problem encountered by any storage method which allocates a fixed amount of memory to each item regardless of its size. But if each entry is not to be allocated a fixed amount of space then the file in which the data is stored will not be divided up in any regular way. This makes it difficult for the program to keep track of the position of individual entries or even to identify where one entry ends and another begins.

Take the following example of two entries in a file which have been allocated precisely the right amount of space:

SMITHJOHN331255645677HIGH STTHOMASBILL45109567851EDEN AV.

You probably had no difficulty in identifying the names of the two men, but your Spectrum is not as familiar as you with common surnames. Even you probably did not guess that each name is followed by the age, file number, telephone number and street number of the man in question. How is the program to identify each of these given that any of them can vary in length?

The answer to such problems is normally provided by a combination of indicators and pointers. Indicators are markers set into the main body of data which allow the program to identify the length of the items which make up an entry. Pointers are normally set outside the main body of data. They consist of a list of the positions, in the memory, of all the entries, enabling the program to jump into the middle of a long and complex file and unerringly find the first character of the desired entry.

The program below uses indicators and pointers to manage a file made up of 28,000 characters, made up of perhaps hundreds of separate entries all packed together in a seemingly random way. The program is called Unifile. I hope it will come to play a valuable part in your program library. More importantly, the techniques employed are essential tools for those who want to pack their Spectrums, 16K or 48K, with the maximum amount of information. The program is dimensioned for use with a 48K version.

MODULE 1.1.1

```
1000 PAPER 7: CLS : BORDER 7: IN
K 6: PAPER 0: PRINT PAPER 2;"
     UNIFILE                   "
1010 PRINT '"FUNCTIONS AVAILABLE
:"
1020 PRINT '"      1)SET UP NEW F
ILE"
1030 PRINT '"      2)ENTER INFORM
ATION"
```

```
1040 PRINT '"      3)SEARCH/DISPL
AY/CHANGE"
1050 PRINT '"      4)STOP"
1060 PRINT ''"PLEASE ENTER WHICH
 YOU REQUIRE."
1070 INPUT Z$
1080 CLS
1090 IF Z$="1" THEN GO SUB 1210
1100 IF Z$="2" THEN GO SUB 1440
1110 IF Z$="3" THEN GO SUB 2180
1120 IF Z$="4" THEN GO SUB 1150
1130 CLS
1140 GO TO 1000
1150 PRINT AT 10,5; INK 7; PAPER
 2;"FILING SYSTEM CLOSED"
1160 BEEP 2,2
1180 INPUT "Have you input new i
nformation  you wish to save? (Y
/N)";Q$: IF Q$="N" THEN STOP
1190 SAVE "UNIFILE": PRINT '"Rew
ind tape, then press any key to
VERIFY": PAUSE 0: VERIFY "UNIFIL
E": STOP
```

As a rule of thumb, a utility program that does not commence with a fairly clear-cut menu of the functions available is a bad program. If you do not agree with this now, you certainly will some time when you have to return to a complex but useful program which you have not used for some time and have to spend hours going through the listing trying to work out just what you have to do to make the program work for you.

In this module the user is requested to choose between four numbered functions. No particular attempt is made to guard against mistaken inputs. Mistakes at this stage are not serious. If a number or character other than 1-4 is input, the program ignores it. The module also contains, as one of the four menu choices, the STOP function. This serves the purpose of marking an end to the use of the program and reminds the user to re-record any new data which has been entered.

Commentary
Line 1000: Every program on the Spectrum which is not going to be in black on white needs to declare somewhere near the start the colours to be used for:
a) The border around the screen
b) The screen
c) The ink with which the characters appear on the screen.

There are three separate PAPER instructions in this line. The first instruction stands alone and, with the CLS command, sets the screen to white. In the second instruction the paper colour is set to black so that the menu stands out boldly from the white background. The third PAPER instruction is tied to a PRINT instruction. It makes no permanent difference to the paper colour, but ensures that the word Unifile is printed on a red background.

It is important that you can distinguish between those colour commands which stand alone and set a colour, and those colour commands which refer only to the single PRINT s、.tement to which they are tied. A single PRINT statement can have every characteristic set by such tied commands. For example:

```
PRINT FLASH 1;OVER 1;INVERSE 1;PAPER 7;INK Ø;"HELLO"
```

None of these colour commands will have any effect on PRINT statements in other parts of the program.

Line 1070: When you have an input to a program menu do remember to check that the variables you use are not duplicated in other parts of the program.

Line 1080: The menu is printed on white paper in bold black strips. But the last PAPER command set the background to black so this CLS command sets the whole screen black. It remains black until the program returns to the menu.

Line 1190: For any data storage program it is far more convenient to have a SAVE instruction built into the program rather than having to enter it in direct mode every time new data has been added.

Testing Module 1.1.1
A rough and ready test of the module is simply to RUN it and enter numbers in the range 1 to 3. The program should then stop with the report 0 OK followed by the appropriate line number from 1090-1110. Input of 4 should result in a prompt to SAVE and then VERIFY the program. Any other input should be ignored.

MODULE 1.1.2

```
2750 REM ************************
2760 REM FUNCTIONAL SUBROUTINES
2770 REM ************************
2780 INPUT Q$
2790 LET Q$=CHR$ (LEN Q$+1 )+Q$
2800 RETURN
2810 PRINT A$( I,2 TO CODE A$( I,1
));":";
2820 RETURN
2830 PRINT FN A$( )( 2 TO )
2840 RETURN
2850 FOR I=1 TO X
2860 GO SUB 2810
2870 GO SUB 2830
2880 LET C=C+CODE B$( C )
2890 NEXT I
2900 RETURN
```

This simple module contains a number of very brief routines which are more economically placed into a subroutine than written out in full every time they are needed. Note the similarity here to the use of a user-defined function which serves a similar space-saving function. If a function is always to work on the same variables then a one line subroutine can be just as effective. Defined functions come into their own when the same function is made to work upon different variables in different places.

Line 2790 could, for instance, be replaced by a defined function such as DEF FN Q$() = CHR$(LEN Q$ + 1) + Q$. To call up this function, however, would always take two lines, INPUT Q$ and LET Q$ = FN Q$() so there would be no real saving compared with the single line necessary to call up the brief subroutine at 2780. If there were three or four different strings on which we wanted to perform this function we could have defined it as DEF FN Q$(Q$) = CHR$(LEN Q$ + 1) + Q$.

The function can now be applied to other strings, simply by putting the required string into the brackets when the function is called up. e.g. LET C$ = FN Q$(C$).

If we wanted to work on C$ with a one line subroutine, then we would need an extra subroutine to deal with C$.

The moral of all this is simply that defining functions just for the sake of it can be a waste of time. Save valuable defined functions for operations which can be applied to different variables in different places.

The module is made up of four subroutines, as follows:
1) Lines 2780-2800. This section adds to the input Q$ the indicator that was mentioned in the introduction. The indicator takes the form of a single character. Remember that each character on the Spectrum has a unique code value; a list of these values can be found in Appendix A of the Spectrum manual. The CHR$ function can be used to select the correct character to match any value between 0 and 255, while the CODE function translates any character into a value between 0 and 255.

Using these two functions it is possible to store values between 0 and 255 in a single character. In the case of our indicators, the single character that is added stores the length of the string, plus one for the indicator itself, so that when the string is packed into the main file of data, the indicator can be used to identify how much of what comes after the indicator is part of the same item. If the indicator has a value of 11 then the item consists of the indicator and the following 10 characters.

2) Lines 2810-2820. These lines print out item names such as name and address. Note that the indicator value is here used to extract the useful part of a line in an array. Item names are stored in A$, whose lines are 20 characters long. The difference between the length of the item name and the length of the line in the array is made up of spaces which we do not wish to print.

Line 2810 prints only that part of the relevant line in A$ which contains the characters of the item name. Neither the indicator nor the spaces are printed. This can be a powerful aid to formatting when text is stored in arrays which are longer than the text.

3) Lines 2830-2840. FN A$ extracts a single item from the main file of data and will be explained further in the next module.

4) Lines 2850-2900. This subroutine is used to print out entries from the file. The variables used will be explained in the discussion of later modules.

Testing Module 1.1.2
The correct performance of these subroutines can only be effectively tested when further modules have been entered.

MODULE 1.1.3

```
1200 REM ************************
1210 REM ENTRY STRUCTURE
1220 REM ************************
1230 PRINT PAPER 2;"        FILE STRUCTURE          "
1240 PRINT '"HOW MANY ITEMS IN EACH ENTRY?"
1250 INPUT X
1260 CLS
1270 DIM A$(X,20)
1280 PRINT PAPER 2;"       NAMES OF ITEMS          "
1290 FOR I=1 TO X
1300 PRINT "ITEM ";I;":";
1310 GO SUB 2780
1320 PRINT Q$(2 TO )
1330 LET A$(I)=Q$
1340 NEXT I
1350 DIM B$(28000)
1360 LET B$(1 TO 4)=CHR$ 2+CHR$ 0+CHR$ 2+CHR$ 255
1370 DEF FN A()=256*CODE Y$(2*S-1)+CODE Y$(2*S)
1380 DEF FN A$()=B$(C TO C+CODE B$(C)-1)
1390 LET P=5
1400 LET Y$=CHR$ 0+CHR$ 1+CHR$ 0+CHR$ 3
1410 LET N=2
1420 RETURN
```

This is the module which permits Unifile to assume different shapes according to the whim of the user. In the course of the module the major arrays and variables are set in preparation for the data to come. Note that one result of this is that any previously stored data is lost. We shall not discuss the use of the various arrays in detail here, preferring to leave that task until we actually begin to use them.

Commentary
Lines 1230-1340. A typical entry to the file might consist of name, address, age and telephone number. In the course of these lines the program records how many such items there will be in each entry in the variable X. The names of the items are requested and stored in the array A$, an indicator having been attached by the subroutine at line 2780. Note that we print Q$ stripped of its first character, since the indicator is not a meaningful character.

Line 1350 is the main array in which the entries will be stored.

Line 1360 sets up two dummy entries which will mark the beginning and end of the file.

Lines 1370-1380. Two examples of user-defined functions which could just as well be replaced by single line subroutines. The first function extracts the value of a pointer and will be explained in the course of Module 5. The second function extracts a single item from the main file based on the value of the indicator found at position C in the file.

Line 1390. P is the variable used to record the first empty space in B$. B$ will always be 28,000 characters long but we will use only part of it. Clearly we need to know how much is already in use.

Line 1400. Y$ stores the pointers in the form of character codes, a method that is discussed in relation to Module 5.

Line 1410. N is the variable which records the number of entries in the file.

Testing Module 1.1.3
We can now test modules 2 and 3. Run the program and select function 1 from the menu. You should be able to specify a number of items and then give them names. Having done this, stop and program and, in direct mode, print out the various arrays and variables as follows:
B$: ??? COPY
Y$: ????
N: 2
P: 5
X should equal the number of items you specified and the array A$ should have X lines, each containing an item name with an indicator tacked on to the front.

MODULE 1.1.4

```
1430 REM ************************
1440 REM NORMAL INPUT
1450 REM ************************
1460 LET R$=""
1470 PRINT PAPER 2;"            EN
TRIES                           "
1480 PRINT '"COMMANDS AVAILABLE:
"
1490 PRINT '">ENTER ITEM SPECIFI
ED"''">""ZZZ"" TO QUIT"
1500 PRINT "*********************
***********"
1510 PRINT "FILE SIZE:";P-1;"/";
LEN B$
1520 FOR I=1 TO X
1530 GO SUB 2810
1540 GO SUB 2780
1580 PRINT Q$(2 TO )
1590 IF Q$(2 TO )="ZZZ" THEN RET
URN
1600 LET R$=R$+Q$
1610 NEXT I
1620 CLS
1630 GO SUB 1660
1640 GO TO 1440
```

The purpose of this module is to accept the input of an entry composed of the correct number of items and to present that entry to the section of the program which will insert it into its correct place in the file.

Commentary
Line 1600. R$ is the entry and is composed of a number of successive Q$s added together.

Testing Module 1.1.4

If you have already entered some sensible item names then start the program with GOTO 1 and call up function 2 from the menu. You should be asked for an input for each item name. After the correct number of item names the program will stop with the report 0 OK,1630:1. The file size should be 4/28000 and, if you print out R$ it should consist of your items, each preceded by an indicator character.

MODULE 1.1.5

```
1650 REM ************************
1660 REM PLACE DATA IN FILE
1670 REM ************************
1680 IF P+LEN R$-1<LEN B$ THEN G
O TO 1730
1690 PRINT AT 14,10;"FILE NOW FU
LL"
1700 PRINT '''    Press any key t
o continue"
1710 PAUSE 0
1720 RETURN
1730 LET POWER=INT (LN (N-1)/LN
2)
1740 LET S=2^POWER
1750 LET T$=R$(2 TO CODE R$(1))
1760 FOR K=POWER-1 TO 0 STEP -1
1770 LET C=FN A()
1780 LET U$=FN A$()(2 TO )
1790 LET S=S+(2^K)*(T$>U$)-(2^K)
*(T$<U$)
1810 IF S>N-1 THEN LET S=N-1
1820 IF S<2 THEN LET S=2
1830 NEXT K
1840 LET C=FN A()
1850 LET U$=FN A$()(2 TO )
1860 IF T$<U$ THEN LET S=S-1
1870 LET B$(P TO P+LEN R$-1)=R$
1880 LET N=N+1
1890 LET Y$=Y$(1 TO 2*S)+CHR$ IN
T (P/256)+CHR$ (P-256*INT (P/256
```

```
))+Y$(2*(S+1)-1 TO )
1900 LET P=P+LEN R$
1910 RETURN
```

This module is the most complex in the program. Before proceeding to a detailed commentary we shall discuss two issues:
1) The use of strings to store numbers
2) The technique of the binary search

Numbers in Strings
We have already seen, in Module 3, that the pointers for our program are stored in a string, Y$. You may be wondering why numeric values are not being stored in a straightforward numeric array. The answer stems from both memory saving and time saving, the latter being the more significant. Let's look at memory saving first.

To cope with the maximum number of entries that are likely to be encountered, a numeric array for the pointers would have to be declared with something like 2,000 elements. It is most unlikely that you will actually have 2,000 entries, but you might. You would have serious problems if your array turned out to have too few spaces for the number of entries that have to be pointed to. An array cannot be re-dimensioned without losing everything in it. The real problem is that a 2,000 element numeric array, because of the way in which Sinclair Basic stores numbers, would occupy some 10,000 bytes of memory. This is an extravagent proportion of the total memory available.

The Spectrum allocates five bytes of memory to every number stored in an array, in an effort to cover as wide a range of numbers as possible — up to 4,294,967,295 in fact. We do not need anything like that range: our file is only 28,000 characters long so we only need whole numbers from 1 to 28,000. Using two character strings it is possible to represent these numbers.

Each character has a code value unique to it, in the range 0 to 255. A single character can be used to store any value between 0 and 255 simply by using the character that has that code. Thus the character A represents the number 65 and the keyword GOTO — just another character as far as the Spectrum is concerned — represents the number 236. Numbers larger than 255 are simply represented by using a second character to store the number of whole 256s, in much the same way that the 3 in 36 means three whole tens in our decimal system. Two characters, therefore, give us the ability to store any positive whole number up to 255*256 + 255. That equals 65,535 and is more than enough to cope with our file of 28,000 characters.

Provided you only want positive whole numbers in the range 0 to 65,535 it is possible to save three of the five bytes that the Spectrum would use if the same numbers were stored in a numeric array.

The catch is that two of the three bytes saved are then thrown away in the search for speed.

Imagine again our numeric array of 2,000 elements and imagine you want to add or delete a number somewhere near the beginning of it. If you simply delete an unwanted value you leave a hole, or rather a zero, in the place where the number once was. If you insert a number you will overwrite what is already there. To avoid either of these unwanted results you have to ensure that every element in the array can be shifted up or down one place. If the position in which you want to insert a new number is position 1, then 1,999 numbers are going to have to be shifted to make room. It can be done with three lines of Basic in the form of a simple loop but it does take time, especially on a Spectrum. Not even its best friends describe the Spectrum as blindingly fast.

Now compare that loop, repeating its operation 1,999 times with this:

```
LET A$="XX" + A$
```

Using the Spectrum's superb string handling we can simply insert two bytes at the beginning, or at the end, or in the middle, of a string with one instruction. This is very fast but it has a drawback — it momentarily doubles the amount of space taken by the string. The Spectrum needs to hold in its memory, even if only for a moment, the new A$ that the line is creating, together with the old A$ that is being used to build it. This limitation is one of the biggest drawbacks to the Spectrum's string handling and it is difficult to avoid. It means that Y$, which is used to store the pairs of characters which we use as pointers to the entries in the main file, is effectively twice as long as it looks since, in our search for speed, it will momentarily double every time we add to it or delete from it. The doubling may only be momentary, but we must still allow memory space for it. It's a shame, but we have to learn to live with it.

This drawback is the reason we do not use the same method for actually inserting or deleting data in our main file B$. To do so would halve the amount of space that could be used for entries. We have set up B$ as a fixed length array and, when we want to delete something, we move the rest of the file down chunk by chunk to fill the gap created.

Binary Searching

We will use the binary search technique to reduce the possible number of comparisons made when finding the correct place to insert a new entry from a possible 12,500 to 15. Consider the following example.

We have established a file which now contains 2,000 items and the current input needs to be inserted at position 1731, although the program has not yet discovered this. The program begins its search by looking at the first entry and comparing it with the new entry to be inserted. The new entry is found to be the greater of the two and so the program moves on to compare it with entry number 2. Eventually after making 1,731 comparisons the program comes across the first entry in the file which is greater than the new entry. It has now found the correct position for the item.

Compare this straightforward procedure with the following for a file of the same size and an insertion in the same position.

The program begins by examining the entry in position 1024, that being the great power of 2 which is less than or equal to the number of entries in the file. The entry at that position is found to be less than the new entry. The program adds 1024/2 to 1024 giving the result 1536. The entry at 1536 is still less than the new entry so 1024/4 is added to 1526, giving 1792. The entry at 1792 is greater than the new entry so 1024/8 is subtracted from 1792 giving 1664. The search proceeds at the following locations in the file with the following additions or subtractions.

1644 (then add 64)
1728 (then add 32)
1760 (then subtract 16)
1744 (then subtract 8)
1736 (then subtract 4)
1732 (then subtract 2)
1730 (then add 1)
Final result: 1731

The power of a binary search should be apparent.

Commentary
Lines 1680-1720. These lines check that there is room in the file for the new entry.

Lines 1730-1830. The binary search is applied to the entries in B$. The search is conducted on the basis of the alphabetical order of the first item in each entry. For an explanation of how the Spectrum understands alphabetical order, see page 95 of the Spectrum manual.

Line 1730 finds the highest power of 2 which is still less than or equal to the number of entries in the file. It uses the logarithm function. The search position is set equal to this.

Lines 1750. T$ is created equal to the first item of the entry in the search position.

Lines 1760-1830. This loop adds or subtracts powers of 2 according to the principles set out in the discussion of binary sorting.

Line 1770. FN A was defined in line 1370. It extracts from two characters in Y$ a numerical value which is a pointer to the first character of an entry in the main file.

Line 1780. FN A$ was defined in line 1380. It extracts from the main files the item whose indicator is found at position C in B$.

Line 1790. This line needs more explanation. A condition such as T$> U$ is either true or false but in everyday usage it cannot be said to have a value in the same way that a number or a variable has value. For the Spectrum, however, T$> U$ has a real value which is either 1, if the condition is true, or 0, if the condition is false. The value of the condition can be used in a program in the same way that a number or a variable can. In this particular line if T$> U$ the condition will have a value of 1 and S will have (2↑K)*1 added to it. On the other hand T$< U$ will equal 0 and S will have (2↑K)*0 subtracted. If T$ had been less than U$ then the roles would have been reversed, while if T$ had been equal to T$ both conditions would have been false and S would not have altered at all.

Lines 1810-1820. If S, the search position, points to one of the dummy entries, these two lines shunt it back into the main body of the data.

Lines 1840-1850. Having completed the binary search, the item at the selected position is extracted for examination. If the item at this position and the new item are equal, the new item is numbered after the existing item. If they are not equal then the new item is numbered before the existing item.

Line 1870. The new entry is added to the end of the file. The correct order of the entries in the file is kept only in Y$. Provided that Y$ knows where the 378th entry is, for instance, it is not important that it is actually stored in the 378th place.

Testing Module 1.1.5

It is difficult to test this module until the search and display function has been added to the program, allowing entries to be displayed with ease. You may care to input a few entries and then stop the program to test whether they have been inserted into B$. Remember that they have been inserted in the order in which they were input. You can also examine Y$ with this loop if you wish.

```
9000 FOR S=1 TO LEN Y$ STEP 2: PRINT FN A():NEXT S
```

This will print out the pointer values, which you should be able to match up with the beginnings of the entries in the main file.

MODULE 1.1.6

```
2170 REM ***********************
2180 REM SEARCH
2190 REM ***********************
2200 LET S=2
2210 PRINT PAPER 2;"
SEARCH               "
2220 PRINT ''"COMMANDS AVAILABLE
:"
2230 PRINT ">INPUT ITEM FOR NORM
AL SEARCH"'">PRECEDE WITH ""SSS"
" FOR"'" SPECIAL SEARCH"'">PRECE
DE WITH ""III"" TO SEARCH"'" FOR
 FIRST CHARACTER OF ENTRY"'">""E
NTER"" FOR FIRST ITEM ON FILE"
2240 PRINT "*********************
************"
2250 PRINT ''"INPUT SEARCH ITEM:
";
2260 GO SUB 2780
2270 PRINT Q$(2 TO )
2280 LET S$=Q$
2290 IF LEN S$=1 THEN GO TO 2510
2300 LET C=FN A( )
2310 IF LEN S$<5 THEN GO TO 2430
2320 IF S$(2 TO 4)<>"III" THEN G
O TO 2390
2330 FOR I=S TO N
2340 LET S=I
2350 LET C=FN A( )
2360 IF B$(C+1)=S$(5) THEN GO TO
 2510
2370 NEXT I
2380 RETURN
```

```
2390 IF S$(2 TO 4)<>"SSS" THEN G
O TO 2430
2400 GO SUB 2920
2410 IF C4=1 THEN GO TO 2510
2420 RETURN
2430 FOR I=1 TO X
2440 IF FN A$()=S$ THEN GO TO 25
10
2450 IF FN A$()=CHR$ 2+CHR$ 255
THEN RETURN
2460 LET C=C+CODE B$(C)
2470 NEXT I
2480 LET S=S+1
2490 LET C=FN A()
2500 GO TO 2430
2510 LET C=FN A()
2520 LET C4=0
2530 IF FN A$()=CHR$ 2+CHR$ 255
THEN RETURN
2540 CLS
2550 PRINT "ENTRY ";S-1;":-"
2560 GO SUB 2850
2570 LET S=S+1
2580 PRINT AT 16,0; PAPER 2;"
     SEARCH                  "
2590 PRINT "COMMANDS AVAILABLE:"
2600 PRINT ">""ENTER"" TO DISPLA
Y NEXT ITEM"'">""ZZZ"" TO QUIT F
UNCTION"'">""AAA"" TO AMEND"'">"
"CCC"" TO CONTINUE SEARCH"
2610 INPUT P$
2620 CLS
2630 IF P$="CCC" THEN GO TO 2300
2640 IF P$="" THEN GO TO 2510
2650 IF P$<>"AAA" THEN GO TO 271
0
2660 LET C=FN A()
2670 CLS
2680 GO SUB 1930
2710 IF P$="ZZZ" THEN RETURN
2720 IF P$="AAA" THEN RETURN
```

```
2730 CLS
2740 GO TO 2260
```

The purpose of this module is to display entries from the file, either one at a time from the beginning or starting from the first entry which satisfies certain search conditions. Having displayed an entry the module gives the user the choice of continuing the search, examining the next entry, changing the entry or deleting it from the file. Note the continuous use of FN A and FN A$ to provide the address of an entry and to extract it from the file.

Commentary
Line 2200. S is the number of the entry currently being examined. It is initially set to 2 because the first entry in the file is actually a dummy.

Lines 2290-2380. If the user inputs a search instruction beginning with III, the program scans the first item of each entry until it finds one which begins with the character following III. If no such item is found the program returns to the main menu.

Lines 2390-2420. The special search which searches for any combination of characters specified, regardless of whether it is a whole item or not, is carried out by a separate subroutine which is called up by these lines if the search instruction begins with SSS.

Lines 2430-2500. Whole items in the file are examined to see whether they correspond to the item the program has been requested to search for. This is much faster than the special search, which moves along the file character by character. A fast binary search cannot be used since only the first items of each entry are in alphabetical order. For this search to be successful the item input must be exactly the same as the item in the memory. Searching for Smith,J in the file would not find Smith,John, whereas using special search, SSSSmith,J would find Smith,J or Smith,John but would be much slower.

Lines 2510-2570. This section prints out an entry using the subroutine at 2850 which we have already examined.

Lines 2580-2740. Having discovered an entry which satisfies the search criteria, the module now offers the user the choice of paging through the file entry by entry, searching for the next entry which satisfies the original search criteria or calling up the routine which allows the entry to be altered or deleted.

Testing Module 1.1.6

You can test the correct functioning of all the search functions with the exception of the special search. The amend function has not yet been entered.

MODULE 1.1.7

```
2910 REM ************************
2920 REM SPECIAL SEARCH
2930 REM ************************
2940 LET C4=0
2950 FOR H=S TO N-1
2960 LET S=H
2970 LET C=FN A( )
2980 LET C1=C
2990 FOR I=1 TO X
3000 LET C1=C1+CODE B$(C1)
3010 NEXT I
3020 FOR J=C+1 TO C1-LEN S$+5
3030 IF B$(J TO J+LEN S$-5)<>S$(
5 TO ) THEN GO TO 3060
3040 LET C4=1
3050 RETURN
3060 NEXT J
3070 NEXT H
3080 LET C4=0
3090 RETURN
```

This module contains the special search routine mentioned above.

Commentary

Line 2940. C4 is the indicator used to show, on return to Module 6, whether the specified combination of characters has been found.

Lines 2980-3010. C1 is first set equal to the start address of the entry under examination. To C1 are added the indicators attached to the X items in the entry, thus making C1 now equal to the start address of the next entry. Note that we are now talking about the start address of the next entry in the main file, not the next entry in alphabetical order.

Lines 3020-3060. The entry is examined character by character for a match with the combination of characters specified in the search instruction.

Testing Module 1.1.7

Enter a series of character combinations, some of which are present in the file and some which are not. Do not forget to precede them with SSS.

MODULE 1.1.8

```
1920 REM ***********************
1930 REM CHANGE ENTRY
1940 REM ***********************
1950 LET S=S-1
1960 LET C=FN A( )
1970 LET R$=""
1980 PRINT "ENTRY ";S-1;":-"
1990 FOR I=1 TO X
2000 GO SUB 2810
2010 GO SUB 2830
2020 PRINT AT 17,0; PAPER 2;"
       AMEND                  "
2030 PRINT "COMMANDS AVAILABLE:"
2040 PRINT ">""ENTER"" LEAVES IT
EM UNCHANGED"'">""ZZZ"" DELETES
WHOLE ENTRY"'">ENTER NEW ITEM"
2050 GO SUB 2780
2060 IF LEN Q$=1 THEN LET R$=R$+
B$(C TO C+CODE B$(C)-1)
2070 LET C=C+CODE B$(C)
2080 CLS
2090 IF LEN Q$=1 THEN GO TO 2120
2100 IF Q$(2 TO )="ZZZ" THEN GO
TO 2130
2110 LET R$=R$+Q$
2120 NEXT I
2130 GO SUB 3130
2140 IF Q$(2 TO )="ZZZ" THEN RET
URN
```

```
2150 GO SUB 1660
2160 RETURN
```

This module gives the user the option of changing or deleting the entry presented to the module by the search function.

Commentary
Lines 2050-2130. You may recall that in Module 4 new entries were constructed in the form of R$. In these lines a modified R$ is created, made up of either items taken directly from the entry in the file, or of items input to replace the originals. The original entry is then deleted from the file by calling up the subroutine at line 3130.

Line 2140. If the user has not specified that the entry is to be deleted, the modified entry, in the form of R$ is presented to Module 5 which inserts it in the correct place.

Testing Module 1.1.8
Full testing of this module must await the entry of the next module, but you can test that the module does display the selected entry item by item and that any changes entered are registered in R$. After displaying all the items of the entry the program will stop with the report 0 OK,2130:1

MODULE 1.1.9

```
3100 REM ************************
3110 REM TELESCOPE FILE
3120 REM ************************
3130 LET C=FN A( )
3140 LET SHIFT=1000
3150 LET C1=C
3160 LET C3=C
3170 FOR I=1 TO X
3180 LET C1=C1+CODE B$(C1)
3190 NEXT I
3200 LET C2=C1-C
3210 FOR I=C1 TO LEN B$-1 STEP S
HIFT
3220 IF LEN B$-I+1<SHIFT THEN LE
T SHIFT=LEN B$-I+1
```

```
3230 LET S$=B$(I TO I+SHIFT-1)
3240 LET B$(C TO C+SHIFT-1)=S$
3250 LET C=C+SHIFT
3260 NEXT I
3270 LET Y$=Y$(1 TO 2*(S-1))+Y$(
2*(S+1)-1 TO )
3280 FOR I=1 TO N-1
3290 LET S=I
3300 LET C=FN A( )
3310 IF C<=C3 THEN GO TO 3350
3320 LET C=C-C2
3330 LET Y$(2*I-1)=CHR$ INT (C/2
56)
3340 LET Y$(2*I)=CHR$ (C-256*INT
 (C/256))
3350 NEXT I
3360 LET P=P-C2
3370 LET N=N-1
3380 RETURN
```

When an entry is deleted from the file, it leaves a gap which must be filled. The function of this module is to delete a specified entry by telescoping the file down over it. The file is not moved entry by entry but in chunks of 1,000 characters.

Commentary
Line 3170. This loop sets C1 to the start address of the next entry.

Lines 3210-3260. This loop shifts 1,000 character chunks of the file downwards the length of the entry to be deleted, the first chunk starting at C1.

Lines 3230-3240. If B$ had been mentioned on both sides of an equation — e.g. LET B$(C TO C + SHIFT – 1) = B$(I TO I + SHIFT – 1) — a shadow of B$ would have been momentarily created and the program would have run out of memory.

Line 3270. The pointer to the deleted entry is removed.

Lines 3280-3350. All the entries which have been shifted down the file must now have their pointers amended since their start addresses are now different.

Testing Module 1.1.9

Use the AMEND function to delete one or two items, then change the first items of some entries in such a way that they must be moved within the file. After each change or deletion, use the SEARCH function to check that the file is still in the correct order. If the tests are satisfactory, the program is now complete.

Summary

You have now completed the input of a substantial and complex program which, I hope, will be of use to you in a variety of circumstances. More important than that, however, you have learned a variety of techniques which will be of use to you in future programs which must handle large amounts of non-numerical data in an economical way.

You have learned how to structure packed data by the use of pointers and indicators. You have seen how strings can be effectively used to store a limited range of numerical data. You have a working example of the powerful binary search technique.

Best of all, if you have taken the trouble to understand what you have been entering, you will have gained confidence that large and complex bodies of data can be processed without the whole thing degenerating into chaos — after all, a major part of the art of programming is having the boldness to jump in and tackle applications which look hopelessly complicated, coupled with the perseverance to follow the task through to the end.

Going Further

If you have understood what you have entered, you might like to tackle some of the following tasks:

1) The program is deliberately written with few multi-statement lines. Once the program is working it would be a good idea to try and shorten it by combining lines — you will learn a great deal about the strengths and weaknesses of multi-statement lines.

2) I have already mentioned that no use is made of the binary search in the actual search module. Why not add another search instruction which refers only to the first item in each entry and which calls up the binary search routine to accomplish the search.

3) The program as structured cannot cope with files or entries which have a variable number of items. This type of structure is quite common. e.g. recipe with title, variable number of ingredients and instructions. It is a fairly simple matter to alter the program so that it works on three items per entry, but with the second item being subdivided into a number of sub-items. The AMEND function should be capable of adding or deleting sub-items.

4) The program makes no provision for sending entries to a ZX printer — this could be easily rectified.

CHAPTER 2

BUILDING A BUDGET — The Spectrum as a Banker
In the last chapter we examined a variety of techniques necessary for the handling of large quantities of non-numeric data. In this chapter we shall be dealing with numbers and, in particular, money.

Three programs are presented in the chapter. The first of them, Budget, is a planning tool for family finance, a program which allows you to examine the consequences of complex financial decisions and to get a picture of how your finances are likely to look over the next 12 months. This is followed by Accountant, a simple program which generates a set of accounts for you in a readable format. Finally, Banker is a program which allows you to keep track of your bank account without waiting for the bank to send you a statement.

2.1 Budget

This is a substantial program, considerably longer than Unifile. This may come as a surprise considering that the amount of information the program handles is considerably less than Unifile's 28,000 characters. There are three main reasons for this. Firstly, Budget is a more flexible program in terms of what it allows the user to do. The list of program functions is far more extensive. Secondly, there is a fair amount of repetitive calculation to be done and it takes space. Thirdly comes the question of formatting. The information stored by the program would be indigestible if it were not for the fact that a large part of the program is given over to ensuring that the data is clearly presented.

MODULE 2.1.1

```
3330 REM ************************
3340 REM QUESTIONS
3350 REM ************************
3360 PRINT AT P1,0;O$
3370 PRINT AT P1,P2;P$
3375 IF H=2 THEN PRINT AT 21,29;
"(H)"
```

```
3380 INPUT Q$
3390 PRINT AT 20,0;O$;O$
3400 PRINT AT 20,0;">>";Q$;"<<"
3410 PRINT AT 21,0;"""ENTER"" to
 confirm"
3420 INPUT R$
3430 PRINT AT 20,0;O$;O$
3440 IF R$="" THEN GO TO 3460
3450 GO TO 3360
3460 LET P2=0
3470 DIM T$(9)
3480 LET T$=Q$
3490 RETURN
```

This may seem a strange place to start but few of the other program modules will function until this one has been inserted. The purpose of the module is to handle almost all the prompts which will be required during the course of the program. This provides a flexible method of formatting them and a simple error checking procedure.

Some programs go to extraordinary lengths to protect against nonsensical inputs which would crash the program or render the results meaningless. These techniques may well contribute to the robustness of a program but they can never make it completely secure against all contingencies. Only experience of a program in use can determine whether it is worth the extra effort to program in such checks.

In this module we adopt the technique of simply reminding the user what has been input and asking for confirmation before it is accepted. The reason that we have an error check in this program when we did not in Unifile is that it is far easier to make a mistake when inputting a series of numbers and yet not be aware that a mistake has been made. This is far more serious than the mis-spelling of a name in an input to a filing program.

Commentary
Line 3360. P1 is simply a line number which is declared before this routine is called up. O$ is a line of 32 blanks: it ensures that the line on which the prompt is to be printed is clear.

Line 3370. P2 is the position along the line. At the start of the program it is set to zero — the beginning of the line — and it stays at zero unless it is changed before this routine is called up. P$ is the text of the current prompt.

Lines 3390-3450. The input is re-printed and the user is asked to confirm that the input was the intended one.

Line 3460. In case P2 has been set to a value other than 0, it is re-set.

Lines 3470-3480. In some cases the input will be compared with a string stored in an array, as in the case of the names of the months. These array lines are nine characters long, regardless of the actual letters in them. The easiest way to make the comparison effective is to set the string input to nine characters too.

Testing Module 2.1.1

You will need to input in direct mode O$,P1,P2 and P$. Now GOTO the Module and it should print out the prompt P$ in the position specified and invite you to confirm your input.

MODULE 2.1.2

```
1000 REM ************************
         THE FIRST TIME THIS
         PROGRAM IS RUN IT WILL
         BE NECESSARY TO ENTER
         IN DIRECT MODE:
         "LET MO=X"
         WHERE X IS THE NUMBER
         OF THE CURRENT MONTH.
1010 REM ************************
1020 LET H=1
1030 DIM O$(32)
1035 LET K$="___________________
_____________"
1040 LET L$="*******************
*************"
1050 DATA "JANUARY","FEBRUARY","
MARCH","APRIL","MAY","JUNE","JUL
Y","AUGUST","SEPTEMBER","OCTOBER
","NOVEMBER","DECEMBER"
1060 DIM N$(12,9)
```

```
1070 RESTORE
1080 FOR I=1 TO 12
1090 READ N$(I)
1100 NEXT I
1180 LET P2=0
1185 CLS
```

This Module sets up the necessary variables. Note the use of the DATA function and its associated commands, READ and RESTORE.

Commentary
Lines 1000-1010. Once you have entered MO for the first time it is probably wise to leave this REM statement in place just in case you inadvertently run the program at some future date and wipe out MO.

Line 1020. This variable will be explained in Module 5.

Lines 1030-1040. These strings are used in formatting the screen.

Lines 1050-1100. The array N$ is filled with the names of the months, using READ, DATA and RESTORE. Note that RESTORE is needed because this program is always started with GOTO 1, which fails to reset the read pointers to the beginning of the data. If the program is run a second time the pointer will have already reached the end of the data and you will get an out of data error report.

Testing Module 2.1.2
This is best done when the other modules using the variables have been entered.

MODULE 2.1.3

```
3590 REM ************************
3600 REM REGISTER MONTH
3610 REM ************************
3615 LET Y=MO+11
3620 PRINT AT 0,10;"HOME BUDGET"
3630 LET P$="WHAT MONTH IS IT?"
3650 LET P1=3
3660 GO SUB 3360
3670 IF T$=N$(MO) THEN RETURN
```

```
3680 FOR I=1 TO 12
3690 IF T$=N$(I) THEN GO TO 3740
3700 NEXT I
3710 CLS
3720 PRINT AT 9,0;"THERE MUST BE
 A MISTAKE IN THE  MONTH YOU GAV
E. I DON'T KNOW OF A MONTH CALLE
D ";Q$;"!"
3730 GO TO 3620
3740 LET M2=I
3750 FOR I=MO TO M2-1+12*(M2<MO)
3755 LET I1=I-12*(I>12)
3760 CLS
3770 PRINT AT 0,11;"UPDATE"
3780 PRINT ''"PLEASE INPUT AMOUN
TS FOR NEXT"'N$(I)
3790 FOR J=1 TO N1
3800 LET P1=5
3830 LET P$=B$(1,J)+":("+STR$ B(
1,J,I1)+"):"
3840 GO SUB 3360
3850 LET B(1,J,I1)=VAL Q$
3860 PRINT AT 5,0;Q$
3870 NEXT J
3900 LET P$="MAIN INCOME:("+STR$
 E(1,I1)+"):"
3910 GO SUB 3360
3920 LET E(1,I1)=VAL Q$
3950 LET P$="ADDITIONAL INCOME:(
"+STR$ E(3,I1)+"):"
3960 GO SUB 3360
3970 LET E(3,I1)=VAL Q$
3980 NEXT I
3990 LET MO=M2
4000 LET Y=MO+11
4010 GO SUB 2600
4015 GO SUB 2900
4020 RETURN
```

The purpose of this module is to check whether the month has changed since the program was last used. If the month has changed, out of date data is deleted and new data is requested. If the change is from May to June the data relating to May is deleted and new data is input for the following May. In this way the period handled by the program always begins with the current month and covers a period of 12 months.

Commentary
Line 3615. Y is the number of the month ending the 12 month period.

Lines 3630-3660. This is an example of how module 1 is called up.

Lines 3670-3730. The month name is compared with the program's current month. If they are not the same the module ascertains the month number or gives an error message.

Lines 3740-4020. This section of the program cannot be tested until some actual data has been entered but its overall purpose is to accept data updating information if the month has changed since the last use.

Line 3750. MO is the number of the last month the program was used. M2 is the number of the current month.

Line 3790. N1 is the total number of payment headings which have been previously input.

Lines 3800-3860. A new figure is requested for each payment heading in turn. As a guide the figure for the month about to be deleted is shown.

Lines 3900-3970. The procedure is repeated for main and additional income.

Line 4010. The subroutine called by this line re-calculates the budgetary analysis.

Testing Module 2.1.3
We can only test whether the module is capable of dealing with month changes and recognising invalid month names. To do this, having entered MO in direct mode, start the program with GOTO 1 and try entering some invalid month names. These should be rejected. Inputting the correct month should result in the module returning — you will need to enter a temporary STOP command at line 3589 to prevent it simply re-executing the module. Try also entering the month after the current month — the program should stop with error report 2, line 3790.

MODULE 2.1.4

```
1510 REM **************************
1520 REM SET UP REGULAR PAYMENTS
1530 REM **************************
1540 DIM B$(2,20,9)
1550 DIM C(20)
1560 DIM B(2,20,12)
1570 DIM D(4,12)
1580 DIM E(4,12)
1590 DIM F(2,12)
1620 LET N1=0
1630 LET N2=0
1635 DIM T(2)
1640 GO SUB 4030
1650 GO SUB 3050
1660 GO SUB 2900
1670 RETURN
```

This module sets up the various arrays used to store the data and requests the initial inputs to those arrays. Note that the calling up of this module results in the loss of any stored data.

Commentary
Line 1540. B$ is the array in which we shall store the names of payment headings: 20 headings are provided for. The first dimension of the array is 2 because the program provides for two parallel sets of data, one of them the real figures and the other a copy to which you can make hypothetical changes without affecting the real data.

Line 1550. C is the array which will hold, for each payment heading, the average monthly payment necessary to fulfil a year's commitment.

Line 1560. The array B will hold the actual monthly payments for the real and hypothetical data.

Line 1570. The array D will hold the total monthly payments for each month. It will also hold an assessment of whether the average monthly budget has in fact covered the amount to be paid out in that month.

Line 1580. The array E holds monthly details of real and hypothetical income.

Line 1590. The array F holds the balance of income over expenditure.

Lines 1620-1630. N1 and N2 refer to the number of payment headings registered in the real and hypothetical sides of the data.

Lines 1640-1660. Having set up the arrays the user is requested to make an initial input of income and payments. These are then copied into the hypothetical side of the array by the subroutine at line 2900.

Testing Module 2.1.4

The testing of this module must wait until the use of the arrays by the other modules.

MODULE 2.1.5

```
1190 GO SUB 3590
1210 PAPER 7: INK 0: CLS : PRINT
 "        HOME BUDGET"
1220 PRINT '"FUNCTIONS AVAILABLE
:"
1230 PRINT PAPER 5;"1)INITIALISE
"
1240 PRINT "2)RESET HYPOTHETICAL
 BUDGET"
1250 PRINT PAPER 5;"3)DISPLAY MO
NTHLY ANALYSIS"
1260 PRINT "4)HYPOTHETICAL ANALY
SIS"
1270 PRINT PAPER 5;"5)REAL CHANG
ES"
1280 PRINT "6)HYPOTHETICAL CHANG
ES"
1290 PRINT PAPER 5;"7)NEW BUDGET
 HEADINGS"
1300 PRINT "8)HYPOTHETICAL BUDGE
T HEADINGS"
1302 PRINT PAPER 5;"9)DELETE REA
L BUDGET HEADING"
1304 PRINT "10)DELETE HYPOTHETIC
```

```
AL HEADING"
1310 PRINT PAPER 5;"11)STOP"
1330 LET P1=15
1340 LET P$="WHICH DO YOU REQUIR
E?"
1350 GO SUB 3360
1360 CLS
1370 LET Z$=Q$
1380 LET H=1+(Z$="2")+(Z$="4")+(
Z$="6")+(Z$="8")+(Z$="10")
1390 IF Z$="1" THEN GO SUB 1520
1400 LET N=N1
1410 IF H=2 THEN LET N=N2
1420 IF Z$="2" THEN GO SUB 2900
1430 IF Z$="3" OR Z$="4" THEN GO
 SUB 1690
1440 IF Z$="5" OR Z$="6" THEN GO
 SUB 4290
1450 IF Z$="7" OR Z$="8" THEN GO
 SUB 3050
1452 IF Z$="9" OR Z$="10" THEN G
O SUB 4870
1460 IF Z$="11" THEN GO TO 1490
1470 CLS
1480 GO TO 1200
1490 PRINT FLASH 1;AT 10,0;"DO Y
OU WISH TO RE-RECORD? (Y/N)": IN
PUT Q$: CLS : IF Q$="Y" THEN SAV
E "BUDGET": BEEP 1,2: PRINT AT 1
0,0;"REWIND, THEN ANY KEY TO VER
IFY": PAUSE 0: VERIFY "BUDGET":
STOP
1500 STOP
```

This is a standard menu module.

Commentary
Line 1380. There are no separate sections of the program to deal with the manipulation of hypothetical data. Each program module works on the real data if H = 1 and on the hypothetical data if H = 2. The line uses logical conditions as variables.

Line 1390. Since there is no reason why there should be the same number of payment headings in the real and hypothetical sections of the data, the variable N is set equal to either N1 or N2 depending on whether H is equal to 1 or 2.

Testing Module 2.1.5
Enter line 3320 and press Return. The program should now accept inputs to this module for all except function 1. Nothing will happen, of course, except that the stop function should work.

MODULE 2.1.6

```
3040 REM ************************
3050 REM INPUT OF PAYMENTS
3060 REM ************************
3070 PRINT "       INPUT OF BILLS"
3080 PRINT ''"PRECEDE NAME OF IT
EM WITH A * IFYOU DO NOT WANT IT
 BUDGETED."
3090 LET P$="HEADING (""ZZZ"" TO
 QUIT):"
3100 LET P1=6
3110 GO SUB 3360
3115 IF Q$="ZZZ" THEN GO SUB 259
0: RETURN
3130 PRINT AT 6,0;P$;Q$
3140 IF H=1 THEN LET N1=N1+1
3150 IF H=2 THEN LET N2=N2+1
3160 LET N=N1*(H=1)+N2*(H=2)
3170 IF N<=20 THEN GO TO 3210
3180 PRINT AT 8,0;"NO MORE ROOM
IN PAYMENTS FILE."
3190 PRINT ''"  Press any key to
 continue."
3195 PAUSE 0
3200 RETURN
```

```
3210 LET B$(H,N)=Q$
3220 FOR I=MO TO Y
3230 LET I1=I-12*(I>12)
3240 LET P$="AMOUNT FOR "+N$(I1)
+":"
3250 LET P1=I+7-MO
3260 GO SUB 3360
3270 LET B(H,N,I1)=VAL Q$
3280 PRINT AT I+7-MO,22;Q$
3290 NEXT I
3300 CLS
3320 GO TO 3070
```

The purpose of the module is to accept new payment headings and to request details of payments under the headings for a 12 month period.

Commentary
Line 3080. Items preceded by an asterisk will not be included in the calculation on the average monthly budget.

Line 3160. Note how the logical conditions are used to increment either N1 or N2.

Line 3120. Note how the value of H is used to determine which half of the array the data is placed into.

Line 3230. If the end of the calendar year has passed, 12 is subtracted from I1 so that it remains in the range 1-12.

Line 3250. The loop value is used to format the printing of successive P$s.

Testing Module 2.1.6
The program should, once initialised, accept payment headings together with associated payments and store them in either the real or the hypothetical sides of the relevant arrays. This can only be checked by printing out elements from the arrays B$ and B in direct mode.

MODULE 2.1.7

```
4030 REM ************************
4040 REM INCOME
4050 REM ************************
4060 PRINT "                INCOME"
4070 PRINT ''"PLEASE INPUT SALAR
Y FOR 12      MONTHS AS FOLLOWS:
"
4080 FOR I=MO TO Y
4090 LET I1=I-12*(I>12)
4100 LET P$=N$(I1)+":"
4110 LET P1=I+5-MO
4120 GO SUB 3340
4130 LET E(H,I1)=VAL Q$
4140 PRINT AT I+5-MO,10;E(H,I1)
4150 NEXT I
4160 CLS
4170 PRINT "NOW INPUT ANY OTHER
ANTICIPATED INCOME:"
4180 FOR I=MO TO Y
4190 LET I1=I-12*(I>12)
4200 LET P1=I+5-MO
4210 LET P$=N$(I1)+":"
4220 GO SUB 3360
4230 LET E(H+2,I1)=VAL Q$
4240 PRINT AT I+5-MO,10;E(H+2,I1
)
4250 NEXT I
4260 CLS
4270 RETURN
```

This module accepts data on income for the 12 months, under the headings of salary and other anticipated income.

Commentary

Lines 4080-4150. This loop accepts the salary figures to be placed in the array E.

Lines 4170-4250. As above but for supplementary income.

Testing Module 2.1.7
This module is accessed via the initialise module, which you should call from the menu. You will be asked to input payment headings then, when you quit with ZZZ, to input income under the two headings. The program should return to the menu after the income figures have been input.

MODULE 2.1.8

```
3500 REM ************************
3510 REM MONEY$
3520 REM ************************
3530 LET M=M+1000.0001*(M>=0)-10
00.0001*(M<0)
3540 LET M$=(STR$ ABS M)(2 TO 4)
3550 IF ABS M>=2000 THEN LET M$=
"***"
3560 IF M<0 THEN LET M$=" "+M$+""
3570 RETURN
```

This module constructs strings out of the stored data representing sums of money. This is done to make the figures easier to format.

Commentary
Line 3530 .1000.0001 is added to ensure there will be three figures before the decimal point and two after it, without altering the value of any figures which may already be in those positions. M is a temporary variable and the process does not affect the value of the original number.

Line 3550. When presenting the data the program can only display the three digits before the decimal point. If this is a serious drawback for you it is a simple method to alter it so that it can display values up to 9999. This limitation does not affect what is stored, only what is displayed.

Line 3560. The program needs to be able to display negative numbers and to make it plain that they are negative. This is done by printing them in inverse video. It is not apparent from the print-out but the string created at the end of the line consists of:

"[4 with CAPS SHIFT]" + M$ + "[3 with CAPS SHIFT]"

The two apparently empty strings which are placed at either end of M$ add two control characters. One sets what follows to inverse video. The other returns to true video.

Testing Module 2.1.8
In direct mode enter LET M = 1 and then GOSUB 3500. Then print out the M$ which has been created. Try this with other values, including some negative numbers.

MODULE 2.1.9

```
2590 REM ************************
2600 REM UPDATE BUDGET
2610 REM ************************
2620 LET T(H)=0
2630 FOR I=1 TO N
2640 LET BUDGET=0
2650 IF B$(H,I,1)="*" THEN GO TO
 2710
2660 FOR J=1 TO 12
2670 LET BUDGET=BUDGET+B(H,I,J)
2680 NEXT J
2690 LET C(I)=BUDGET/12
2700 LET T(H)=T(H)+C(I)
2710 NEXT I
2720 LET TTOTAL=0
2730 LET CUM=0
2740 FOR I=MO TO Y
2750 LET I1=I-12*(I>12)
2760 LET D(H,I1)=0
2770 FOR J=1 TO N
2780 LET D(H,I1)=D(H,I1)+B(H,J,I
1)
2790 NEXT J
2800 LET TTOTAL=TTOTAL+D(H,I1)
2810 FOR J=1 TO N
2820 IF B$(H,J,1)="*" THEN LET T
```

```
TOTAL=TTOTAL-B(H,J,I1)
2830 NEXT J
2840 LET D(H+2,I1)=T(H)*(I-MO+1)
-TTOTAL
2850 LET CUM=CUM+E(H,I1)+E(H+2,I
1)-D(H,I1)
2860 LET F(H,I1)=CUM
2870 NEXT I
2880 RETURN
```

This module performs the calculations which provide the variety of analyses of income and expenditure. It is in fact far less complex than it looks since all that is involved is simple addition, subtraction and division by 12.

Commentary
Line 2620. T is a two element array which is used to store the sum of the individual monthly budget payments to give an overall monthly budget.

Lines 2630-2710. In this loop the total yearly payments for each payment heading are found and divided by 12 to give a monthly average. The array C stores the monthly average for each payment heading. Note that payment names beginning with "*" are exempted from this procedure.

Line 2740-2790. The array D is loaded with the total of payments for each month.

Lines 2800-2840. The total of payments in each month is stored in the array D. These sums are cumulated in TTOTAL and from TTOTAL are subtracted any payments the user did not want included in the average budget. For each run through the loop beginning at 2740, TTOTAL is set to contain the total payments, up to and including month I1, which belong to payment headings included in the average monthly budget. In line 2840 TTOTAL is subtracted from I1 times the average monthly budget. The resulting figure is the balance of the monthly budget up to that month over the total of payments for budgeted items. This is stored in the second half of the array D. And if that all sounds as confusing to you as it does to me, have faith and wait until you have the chance to display a few simple figures and then read it again.

Line 2850. The balance of income over expenditure is stored as CUM and this is stored as successive elements of the array F.

Testing Module 2.1.9
This module will be tested after the entry of the next module.

MODULE 2.1.10

```
1680 REM ************************
1690 REM DISPLAY BILLS
1700 REM ************************
1710 PRINT "           PAYMENTS"
1720 LET P$="MONTH TO START"
1730 LET P1=3
1740 GO SUB 3360
1750 FOR I=1 TO 12
1760 IF T$=N$(I) THEN GO TO 1790
1770 NEXT I
1780 GO TO 1720
1790 LET M1=I
1800 IF MO-M1+12*(M1>MO-1)<4 THE
N LET M1=MO-4+12*(MO<5)
1810 CLS
1820 PRINT "MONTH            _  _  _
 _   _ B _"
1830 OVER 1: PRINT AT 0,0;TAB 10
;N$(M1, TO 3);TAB 14;N$(M1+1-12*
(M1>11), TO 3);TAB 18;N$(M1+2-12
*(M1>10), TO 3);TAB 22;N$(M1+3-1
2*(M1>9), TO 3)'L$: OVER 0
1840 FOR I=1 TO N
1843 PAPER 5: IF I/2<>INT (I/2)
THEN PAPER 7
1850 IF I<>11 THEN GO TO 1920
1860 PRINT AT 20,0;"PRESS ANY KE
Y TO CLS & CONTINUE"
1870 PAUSE 0
1880 FOR J=2 TO 21
1890 PRINT AT J,0;O$
1900 NEXT J
1910 PRINT AT 2,0;
1920 PRINT B$(H,I);"_";
1930 FOR J=M1 TO M1+3
```

```
1940 LET M=B(H,I,J-12*(J>12))
1950 GO SUB 3500
1960 PRINT M$;"_";
1970 NEXT J
1980 LET M=C(I)
1990 GO SUB 3500
2000 PRINT M$;"_"
2010 GO SUB 3500
2020 NEXT I
2030 PRINT K$
2040 PRINT ''"PRESS ANY KEY FOR
ANALYSIS"
2050 PAUSE 0
2070 FOR I=2 TO 21
2080 PRINT AT I,0;O$
2090 NEXT I
2110 PAPER 5: PRINT AT 2,0;"TOTA
L      _"''"BUDG.BAL._"''"OTHER IN
C_"''"CASH BAL._"
2115 PAPER 7: PRINT AT 3,0;"BUDG
ET     _"''"PAY         _"''"TOTAL IN
C_"''"CUM. BAL._"
2130 FOR I=M1 TO M1+3
2140 OVER 1: PRINT AT 2,0;
2150 LET I1=I-12*(I>12)
2160 LET I2=10+4*(I-M1)
2170 LET M=D(H,I1)
2180 GO SUB 3500
2190 PAPER 5: PRINT TAB I2;M$;"_
"
2200 LET M=T(H)
2210 GO SUB 3500
2220 PAPER 7: PRINT TAB I2;M$;"_
"
2230 LET M=D(H+2,I1)
2240 GO SUB 3500
2280 PAPER 5: PRINT TAB I2;M$;"_
"
2290 LET M=E(H,I1)
2300 GO SUB 3500
2310 PAPER 7: PRINT TAB I2;M$;"_
"
```

```
2320 LET M=E(H+2,I1)
2330 GO SUB 3500
2340 PAPER 5: PRINT TAB I2;M$;"__
"
2350 LET M=E(H,I1)+E(H+2,I1)
2360 GO SUB 3500
2370 PAPER 7: PRINT TAB I2;M$;"__
"
2380 LET M=(E(H,I1)+E(H+2,I1)-D(
H,I1))
2400 GO SUB 3500
2440 PAPER 5: PRINT TAB I2;M$;"__
"
2450 LET M=F(H,I1)
2460 GO SUB 3500
2500 PAPER 7: PRINT TAB I2;M$;"__
"
2510 NEXT I
2520 OVER 0: PRINT K$( TO 28)
2530 LET P$="DO YOU WISH TO SEE
FIGURES        AGAIN? (Y/N):"
2540 LET P1=20
2550 GO SUB 3360
2560 IF Q$<>"Y" THEN RETURN
2570 CLS
2580 GO TO 1810
```

The purpose of this rather daunting looking module is to display the various data and analyses in tabular form. Of particular interest is the way in which the table is largely formatted on the basis of variables already occurring within the program — if data has a regular structure it can be made to dictate the format of its presentation without too much difficulty.

Commentary

Lines 1700-1810. This section accepts the input of a start month for the table and tests it for validity. The start month can never be later than month 9 of the 12 month period as four months are displayed.

Line 1820-1830. These two lines print out the heading of the table, including the first three letters of the month name.

Lines 1840-2020. This loop prints out the payment headings and the monthly payments associated with them for the four month period. To make the separate lines of the table stand out the paper colour is varied according to whether the loop variable is odd or even.

Lines 2060-2090. Using a line of empty spaces and a loop is an effective way of clearing a part of the screen.

Lines 2110-2510. This section prints out the various analyses of income and expenditure. Note how the loop variable is used (2150,2160) to create two further variables on which the formatting of the data is based. After the printing of the headings in lines 2110-2120, examination of the following lines shows that they fall into eight sections. Each section begins with the setting up of the temporary variable M and the calling of Module 8, followed by the printing of M$.

Testing Module 2.1.10

Clear any data already stored, enter MO again in direct mode and start the program with GOTO 1. Enter income and some payments but keep them simple — whole tens or hundreds. Call up Module 3 and examine the result. If there is a problem with the formatting then you have probably made an error in the entry of Module 10. If the figures do not make sense the error is probably in Module 9. If it is the actual payments that are wrong, look at the payments input in Module 6. For errors in the income figures inspect Module 7.

MODULE 2.1.11

```
2890 REM ************************
2900 REM SET UP SHADOW ARRAY
2910 REM ************************
2920 FOR I=1 TO N1
2930 LET B$(2,I)=B$(1,I)
2940 FOR J=1 TO 12
2950 LET B(2,I,J)=B(1,I,J)
2960 LET D(2,J)=D(1,J)
2970 LET D(4,J)=D(3,J)
2980 LET E(2,J)=E(1,J)
2990 LET E(4,J)=E(3,J)
2995 LET F(2,J)=F(1,J)
```

```
3000 NEXT J
3010 NEXT I
3020 LET N2=N1
3030 RETURN
```

This module copies the data from the real half of the array into the hypothetical half. If there was any difference between the real and hypothetical halves then it is lost if this function is used.

Testing Module 2.1.11

You are now in a position to test that there is a proper separation between the real and hypothetical data areas. Enter some new hypothetical payments, check that they have been accepted by calling up function 4 on the menu and then return to the menu and call up function 3. The table displayed should bear no trace of the hypothetical payments you have entered.

MODULE 2.1.12

```
4280 REM ************************
4290 REM CHANGES
4300 REM ************************
4310 PRINT "                  CHANGES
"
4320 PRINT ''"1)CHANGE EXISTING
BUDGET HEAD"'"2)CHANGE MAIN INCO
ME"'"3)CHANGE ADDITIONAL INCOME"
4340 LET P$="WHICH DO YOU REQUIR
E?"
4350 LET P1=7
4360 GO SUB 3360
4370 LET H$=Q$
4380 CLS
4410 IF H$="1" THEN GO SUB 4460
4420 IF H$="2" OR H$="3" THEN GO
 SUB 4690
4440 GO SUB 2600
4450 RETURN
4460 LET P$="NAME OF BUDGETARY H
```

```
EADING TO BE CHANGED ?"
4470 LET P1=1
4480 GO SUB 3340
4490 FOR I=1 TO N
4500 IF T$=B$(H,I) THEN GO TO 45
60
4510 NEXT I
4520 PRINT ''" NO HEADING OF THA
T NAME."''"  Press any key to co
ntinue."
4530 PAUSE 0
4550 RETURN
4560 LET B=I
4570 LET P$="NEW FIGURE OR ""Z""
 TO LEAVE."
4580 LET P1=17
4590 FOR I=MO TO Y
4600 LET I1=I-12*(I>12)
4610 PRINT AT I-MO+3,0;N$(I1);":
";B(H,B,I1)
4620 GO SUB 3340
4630 IF Q$="Z" THEN GO TO 4660
4640 LET B(H,B,I1)=VAL Q$
4650 PRINT AT I-MO+3,15;"(";B(H,
B,I1);")"
4660 NEXT I
4670 GO SUB 2590
4680 RETURN
4730 LET X=2*(H$="3")
4750 PRINT "MAIN INCOME:" AND (H
$="2");"SUPPLEMENTARY INCOME:" A
ND (H$="3")
4760 LET P$="INPUT NEW FIGURE OR
 ""Z"" TO LEAVE"
4770 LET P1=17
4780 FOR I=MO TO Y
4790 LET I1=I-12*(I>12)
4800 PRINT AT I+3-MO,0;N$(I1);":
";E(H+X,I1)
4810 GO SUB 3340
4820 IF Q$="Z" THEN GO TO 4850
```

```
4830 LET E(H+X,I1)=VAL Q$
4840 PRINT AT I-MO+3,15;"(";E(H+
X,I1);")"
4850 NEXT I
4860 RETURN
```

This module allows changes to be made to existing data.

Commentary
Lines 4460-4680. Current monthly payments under a specified payment heading are displayed and may be confirmed or altered. Budgetary analysis is then re-calculated.

Lines 4730-4860. A variable X is set according to whether main or additional income has been specified. Figures input are stored in the relevant section of the array E according to the value of X.

Testing Module 2.1.12
Call up the module and make some changes to the existing data, both real and hypothetical.

MODULE 2.1.13

```
4870 REM ************************
4880 REM DELETE BUDGET HEAD
4890 REM ************************
4900 LET P$="NAME OF ITEM TO BE
DELETED?"
4910 LET P1=1
4920 GO SUB 3340
4930 FOR I=1 TO N
4940 IF T$=B$(H,I) THEN GO TO 50
00
4950 NEXT I
4960 PRINT AT 2,8;"ITEM NOT FOUN
D."''" Press any key to continue
."
```

```
4970 PAUSE 0
4980 RETURN
5000 IF H=1 THEN LET N1=N-1
5010 IF H=2 THEN LET N2=N-1
5015 LET N=N1*(H=1)+N2*(H=2)
5020 FOR J=I TO N
5030 LET B$(H,J)=B$(H,J+1)
5040 FOR K=1 TO 12
5050 LET B(H,J,K)=B(H,J+1,K)
5060 NEXT K
5070 NEXT J
5120 GO SUB 2600
5130 RETURN
```

This module defines an existing payment heading from the real or hypothetical area, together with its associated payments.

Commentary
Lines 4930-4980. The name of the item to be deleted is compared with existing payment headings.

Lines 5000-5120. N1 or N2 is decremented according to whether the deletion is from the real or hypothetical data. Items in B$ and B are then shifted down one at a time to overwrite the position of the data to be deleted. The budgetary analysis is re-calculated.

Testing Module 2.1.13
Testing is achieved by simply deleting some headings. If the deletions work the program is correctly entered and ready for use.

Summary
This long program is a powerful tool, properly used, although it takes some practice to get the most out of it. Taken seriously it can give you some quite surprising information about the state of your finances over the year to come — when things will be tight and when there might be a bit to spread around, how payments could be re-arranged to ensure a bit extra for Christmas or holidays, what would be the overall effect of a new commitment or an increase in income.

This is not the end of it, however. With not too much adaptation the framework of the program could be applied to a variety of uses where data must be displayed and analysed under a variety of headings, where it needs to be changed at will and where it must be possible to make hypothetical entries or changes without corrupting the existing data.

With changes to Module 9 the program can easily be made to perform very different calculations to the ones specified here. Remember that it is not the individual Basic lines that are the most difficult to get working when you tackle a new application — it is getting them to work together. Once this program is working to your satisfaction, with any improvements you may want to make, look upon it as a framework for your own ideas and tasks, rather than as something which can only ever be applied to your family budget.

In addition, you should have gained some confidence in entering this program in the technique of handling and sub-dividing large arrays by the simple use of variables within the program. You have practical examples of the way in which loop variables and other variables can be used to aid the formatting of data.

Lastly, you have an example of a simple module for the formatting and checking of program prompts, a potential boon in interactive programs.

Going Further

1) Like Unifile this program is written with hardly any use of multi-statement lines. Shorten the program as much as you can by combining individual lines.

2) Except where absolutely necessary for clarity of presentation, no attempt has been made to make the output of the program interactive in colour terms. Go through the program and brighten it up with some colour commands in the right places.

3) Take a look at the arrays defined in Module 4. Several of them could easily be combined together. This could result in a big saving when printing out the table of analyses since the module could simply work methodically through one array rather than referring to 4 or 5. Try it and see.

2.2 Accountant

This simple program allows the user to create neat and comprehensible accounts easily. No analysis is performed except to generate sub-totals and totals where appropriate, so if the books do not balance you will have to sort it out yourself. Since the program is quite simple the commentaries on the modules are much shorter than before.

MODULE 2.2.1

```
1000 REM ***********************
1010 REM MENU
1020 REM ***********************
1030 PAPER 7: INK 0: CLS : PRINT
 "               ACCOUNTS"
1040 PRINT '"FUNCTIONS AVAILABLE
:"
1050 PRINT '"1)INPUT NEW HEADING
S"
1060 PRINT '"2)CHANGE AMOUNTS/DE
LETE ITEMS"
1070 PRINT '"3)PRINT ACCOUNTS"
1080 PRINT '"4)INITIALISE ACCOUN
TS"
1090 PRINT '"5)STOP"
1100 INPUT Z$
1110 CLS
1120 IF Z$<>"4" AND Z$<>"5" THEN
 GO SUB 1320
1130 CLS
1140 IF Z$="1" THEN GO SUB 1390
1150 IF Z$="2" THEN GO SUB 2120
1160 IF Z$="3" THEN GO SUB 2660
1170 IF Z$="4" THEN GO SUB 1210
1180 IF Z$="5" THEN GO TO 1202
1190 CLS
1200 GO TO 1000
1204 PRINT FLASH 1;AT 10,10;"ACC
OUNTANT": INPUT "Do you want to
re-record? (Y/N)";Q$: IF Q$="Y"
THEN SAVE "ACCOUNTANT": BEEP 1,2
: PRINT AT 10,0;"REWIND, THEN AN
Y KEY TO VERIFY.": VERIFY "ACCOU
NTANT"
1208 STOP
```

This is a standard program menu.

MODULE 2.2.2

```
1210 REM ************************
1220 REM CREDIT/DEBIT
1230 REM ************************
1240 DIM A$(2,100,15)
1250 DIM A(2,100)
1260 DIM C(2)
1270 LET C(1)=1
1280 LET C(2)=1
1290 DIM O$(32)
1300 LET L$="--------"
1310 RETURN
```

This module initialises the variables involved and will result in the loss of any previously stored data.

Commentary
Line 1240. A$ will hold the names of headings in two sections, one for credits and the other for debits.

Line 1250. The array will hold the figures corresponding to the headings in A$.

Lines 1260-1280. C will hold the number of items stored in the credit and debit areas.

MODULE 2.2.3

```
1320 REM ************************
1330 REM CREDIT OR DEBIT?
1340 REM ************************
1350 PRINT AT 10,3;"DO YOU WANT:
1)CREDIT"
1360 PRINT "                    2)DEB
IT"
```

```
1370 INPUT CD
1380 RETURN
```

This module sets the variable CD according to whether the user wishes to deal with the credit or the debit side of the data.

Testing Module 2.2.3

Any function selected from the menu should result in this module being called.

MODULE 2.2.4

```
1390 REM ************************
1400 REM INPUT ITEMS
1410 REM ************************
1430 PRINT "               NEW ITEMS"
1440 PRINT '"IS THE ITEM:1)A SIN
GLE ITEM"
1450 PRINT "               2)A MAIN
 HEADING"
1460 PRINT "               3)A SUB-
HEADING"
1470 PRINT '"              ""0"" TO
 QUIT FUNCTION"
1480 INPUT TYPE
1490 IF TYPE=0 THEN RETURN
1500 IF TYPE=3 THEN GO TO 1750
```

This module is used to specify the type of the heading that is about to be stored in the accounts. There are three types:

1) Single items which will be entered straight into the main column of the accounts.

2) Main headings, which have no figures attached to them but act as markers for groups of: — 3) Sub-headings, which will be indented and sub-totalled separately from the main column of figures.

MODULE 2.2.5

```
1510 REM ************************
1520 REM SINGLE ITEM OR MAIN
         HEADING
1530 REM ************************
1540 LET Q=0
1550 PRINT AT 8,0;"NAME OF ITEM
?";
1560 INPUT Q$
1570 PRINT Q$
1580 IF TYPE=2 THEN GO TO 1620
1590 PRINT '"AMOUNT FOR ITEM? ";
1600 INPUT Q
1610 PRINT Q
1620 INPUT "Is this correct? (Y/
N)";R$
1640 IF R$="Y" THEN GO TO 1690
1650 FOR I=8 TO 14
1660 PRINT AT I,0;O$
1670 NEXT I
1680 GO TO 1550
1690 LET Q$=" "+Q$
1700 IF TYPE=2 THEN LET Q$(1)="*
"
1710 LET A$(CD,C(CD))=Q$
1720 LET A(CD,C(CD))=Q
1730 LET C(CD)=C(CD)+1
1735 CLS
1740 GO TO 1410
```

This module accepts the input of main headings or single items as defined above.

Commentary
Lines 1540-1700. An item name is accepted together with an amount if the variable TYPE is set at 1 — indicating a single item. If TYPE is set at 2 then "*" is added to the front of the heading as a marker that it is a main heading.

Lines 1710-1740. If the item is not a main heading, the variable Q now contains the amount of the item. In this section the heading is stored in A$ and the amount in A. Depending on whether the item is a credit or a debit, one of the values in C is incremented.

Testing Module 2.2.5

Input some headings of both types and check that they have been stored in A$, together with the amount in A. The arrays must, of course, have been set up by the initialising module.

MODULE 2.2.6

```
1750 REM ************************
1760 REM SUB-HEADING
1770 REM ************************
1780 PRINT '"NAME OF MAIN HEADIN
G? ";
1790 INPUT Q$
1800 PRINT Q$
1810 LET Q$="*"+Q$
1812 DIM T$(15)
1814 LET T$=Q$
1820 FOR I=1 TO C(CD)
1830 IF A$(CD,I)=T$ THEN GO TO 1
890
1840 NEXT I
1850 PRINT '"SORRY NO HEADING OF
 THAT NAME."
1860 PRINT ''"Press any key to c
ontinue.": PAUSE 0
1880 RETURN
1890 LET PLACE=I+1
1900 PRINT '"NAME OF SUB-HEADING
?";
1910 INPUT Q$
1920 PRINT Q$
1930 PRINT '"AMOUNT FOR SUB-HEAD
ING?";
1940 INPUT Q
1950 PRINT Q
1960 INPUT "Are these correct? (
```

```
Y/N)";R$
1980 IF R$="Y" THEN GO TO 2030
1990 FOR I=8 TO 16
2000 PRINT AT I,0;O$
2010 NEXT I
2015 PRINT AT 8,0;
2020 GO TO 1900
2030 LET Q$="£"+Q$
2040 FOR I=C(CD)+1 TO PLACE+1 ST
EP -1
2050 LET A$(CD,I)=A$(CD,I-1)
2060 LET A(CD,I)=A(CD,I-1)
2070 NEXT I
2080 LET A$(CD,PLACE)=Q$
2090 LET A(CD,PLACE)=Q
2100 LET C(CD)=C(CD)+1
2105 CLS
2110 GO TO 1410
```

To accept sub-headings as defined above.

Commentary
Lines 1750-1890. The name of the relevant main heading is input, checked against the headings already stored and the position of the relevant main heading is stored in the variable PLACE.

Lines 1900-2030. The name of the new sub-heading and the amount are input and confirmed by the user.

Lines 2040-2100. A space is created by moving all the items from position PLACE onwards one space up the array. The new sub-heading is then placed immediately after the relevant main heading.

Testing Module 2.2.6
Input a sub-heading under one of the main headings you entered when testing the last module. Check that the heading and the associated amount have been placed into the relevant arrays.

MODULE 2.2.7

```
2980 REM ************************
2990 REM CREATE M$
3000 REM ************************
3005 LET M=M+.001
3010 LET M$=(STR$ M)( TO LEN STR
$ M-1)
3080 RETURN
```

This module produces a standardised string with two decimal places from the figures attached to the various headings. Unlike the similar module in the previous program, no zeroes are added to the beginning of the number.

MODULE 2.2.8

```
2660 REM ************************
2670 REM PRINT ACCOUNTS
2680 REM ************************
2690 PRINT AT 0,12;"CREDIT" AND
CD=1;AT 1,12;"DEBIT" AND CD=2
2700 LET TTOTAL=0
2710 LET STOTAL=0
2720 FOR I=1 TO C(CD)-1
2730 IF I>1 AND A$(CD,I,1)<>"£"
THEN PRINT
2740 LET TTOTAL=TTOTAL+A(CD,I)
2750 IF A$(CD,I,1)="£" THEN PRIN
T TAB 2;
2760 PRINT A$(CD,I,2 TO );
2770 IF A$(CD,I,1)="*" THEN GO T
O 2850
2780 IF A(CD,I)=0 THEN GO TO 285
0
2790 LET M=A(CD,I)
2800 GO SUB 2980
```

```
2810 PRINT TAB 25-LEN M$;
2820 IF A$(CD,I,1)<>"£" THEN PRI
NT TAB 32-LEN M$;
2830 IF A$(CD,I,1)="£" THEN LET
STOTAL=STOTAL+A(CD,I)
2840 PRINT M$
2850 IF STOTAL=0 OR A$(CD,I+1,1)
="£" THEN GO TO 2910
2860 PRINT TAB 18;L$
2870 LET M=STOTAL
2880 GO SUB 2980
2890 PRINT TAB 25-LEN M$;M$
2900 LET STOTAL=0
2910 NEXT I
2920 LET M=TTOTAL
2930 GO SUB 2980
2950 PRINT '"TOTAL:";TAB 32-LEN
M$;M$
2960 PRINT '"Press any key to co
ntinue."
2965 PAUSE 0
2970 RETURN
```

The purpose of the module is to print out either the credit or the debit side of the accounts.

Commentary

Line 2690. Note the use of AND to control what is printed here. When two items are connected by AND, they take on the value of the first item of the pair if the second item of the pair has a positive value. We have already seen that conditions such as CD = 2 have a value of either 1 or 0 according to whether they are true or false. Accordingly, in this line, if CD = 1 then the expression "CREDIT" AND CD = 1 takes on the value "CREDIT". If CD is not 1 then the expression has no value and nothing is printed. This is an extremely economical way of making choices between items to be printed. (For more information on the strange behaviour of logical expressions, see chapter 13 of the Sinclair manual.)

Lines 2700-2710. These two variables will be used to record the totals of the various groups of sub-headings and the overall total.

Lines 2720-2910. In this loop, each entry of A$ is examined in turn to see whether it is a single item, a main heading or a sub-heading. If it is a single item the heading is printed and the amount entered in the main column. If it is a main heading then no corresponding amount is printed. If it is a sub-heading then the heading is indented by two spaces and the amount associated with it is printed in a separate column before the main column. At the end of each group of sub-headings the total of the group is printed at the foot of the group.

Testing Module 2.2.8
Enter some headings and have them printed out. All decimal points in the main column should be in line.

MODULES 2.2.9

```
2120 REM ************************
2130 REM CHANGES AND DELETIONS
2140 REM ************************
2150 FOR I=1 TO C(CD)-1
2160 PRINT AT 0,10;"CHANGE OR DE
LETE"
2170 IF A$(CD,I,1)<>"£" THEN PRI
NT AT 3,0;O$
2180 PRINT AT 5,0;O$
2190 IF A$(CD,I,1)<>"£" THEN PRI
NT AT 3,0;A$(CD,I,2 TO )
2200 IF A$(CD,I,1)="£" THEN PRIN
T AT 5,0;A$(CD,I,2 TO )
2210 IF A(CD,I)=0 THEN GO TO 225
0
2220 LET M=A(CD,I)
2230 GO SUB 2980
2240 PRINT TAB 16;M$
2250 PRINT AT 18,0;">ENTER=NEXT
ITEM"
2260 PRINT ">""CCC""=CHANGE AMOU
NT"
2270 PRINT ">""ZZZ""=QUIT FUNCTI
ON"
2280 PRINT ">""DDD""=DELETE ITEM
"
2290 INPUT Q$
2300 IF Q$="ZZZ" THEN RETURN
```

```
2310 IF Q$="DDD" THEN GO SUB 246
0: RETURN
2325 IF Q$="" THEN GO TO 2440
2330 PRINT AT 18,0;O$;O$;O$;O$
2340 PRINT AT 18,0;"AMOUNT TO BE
 ADDED?";
2350 INPUT Q$
2360 PRINT Q$
2370 INPUT "Is that correct? (Y/
N)";R$
2390 PRINT AT 18,0;O$;O$;O$;O$
2400 IF R$="N" THEN GO TO 2340
2410 LET A(CD,I)=A(CD,I)+VAL Q$
2420 PRINT AT 6,0;O$
2430 GO TO 2160
2440 NEXT I
2450 RETURN
```

This module allows the user to change the amounts associated with items already entered into the accounts. There is no search function attached to the module; the user simply pages through the items in the account until the right one is reached. The amount associated with an item is changed by inputting an amount which is to be added to the currently stored amount. This is on the assumption that alterations will normally be for the purpose of registering extra spending or income under existing headings. If you wish to subtract, simply input a negative number.

Testing Module 2.2.9
Try changing a number of items then displaying their new values.

MODULE 2.2.10

```
2460 REM ***********************
2470 REM DELETE ITEM
2480 REM ***********************
2490 LET PLACE=I
2500 LET DELETION=1
```

```
2510 IF A$(CD,PLACE,1)<>"*" THEN
 GO TO 2550
2520 LET DELETION=0
2530 LET DELETION=DELETION+1
2540 IF A$(CD,PLACE+DELETION,1)=
"£" THEN GO TO 2530
2550 FOR K=PLACE TO C(CD)-DELETI
ON-1
2560 LET A$(CD,K)=A$(CD,K+DELETI
ON)
2565 LET A(CD,K)=A(CD,K+DELETION
)
2570 NEXT K
2580 LET C(CD)=C(CD)-DELETION
2650 RETURN
```

This module deletes items from the accounts. If the item to be deleted is a main heading, all its associated sub-headings are also deleted.

Commentary
Lines 2490-2540. If the item to be deleted is a main heading the variable DELETION is incremented until it is equal to the main heading and the number of its sub-headings.

Lines 2550-2580. The items higher up the array are moved down to cover the items to be deleted. The variable recording the number of items is decremented by the number of items deleted.

Testing Module 2.2.10
Delete some items and check that this has been effective. The program is now ready for use.

Going Further
1) Why not try adding some more interesting colours?
2) Try adding a function which calculates a balance and includes it in one or other side of the accounts.

3) If there were actually 50 or more items on one side of the accounts it would take far too long paging through them to make alterations. Try adding a search function which allows the user to input a number and then jumps forward or even backwards that number of items.

2.3 The Banker

In this program we start to make extensive use of multi-statement lines. The program is a neat little tool which allows you to keep your own financial records in much the same format as a bank statement. It deals with recurring payments, either regular or irregular ones, and inserts them into the statement on the right day in every month in which they occur.

The program is a simple one, but compared to what has gone before it is not as short as it looks. It would be 50% longer if it were not for the fact that multi-statement lines are used.

One of the things to watch out for as you enter the program is the use of IF statements. Such statements are capable of causing havoc if used improperly in multi-statement lines, creating program bugs which are extremely difficult to trace. Equally, multi-statement lines can be used to increase the effectiveness and the ease with which IF statements are used. The reason for this is that if the condition specified by an IF statement is not met, the program does not simply skip over that part of the line containing the IF statement, it skips the whole of the rest of the line.

In other words, any statements after the IF statement will only be executed if the IF statement is true. This is so different from the behaviour of single-statement lines that it is easy to forget.

The advantage of this is that it provides a form of automatic and elegant GOTO which you do not even have to specify. If you have a series of ten operations which are to be performed together provided, say, that C = 1 at some point, then with single-statement lines you would have to place an IF statement at the beginning of the section to specify a jump around the section if C is not equal to 1. It works but it does feel messy and it is difficult to read a program where there are a lot of jumps.

With multi-statement lines, however, you could begin a single line with IF C = 1 and follow it with ten operations. Not only would this work and save memory, it would actually make the program more readable in many ways since it would be immediately clear that the ten operations formed a logical unit.

MODULE 2.3.1

```
1000 REM ************************
1010 REM MENU
1020 REM ************************
1030 CLS : INK 0: PAPER 7: PRINT
 AT 0,10; INK 2; FLASH 1;"BANKER
"
1040 PRINT '"1)NEW PAYMENTS"
1050 PRINT '"2)EXAMINE/DELETE PA
YMENTS"
1060 PRINT '"3)PRINT STATEMENT"
1070 PRINT '"4)INITIALISE"
1080 PRINT '"5)STOP"
1090 INPUT Z$: CLS
1100 IF Z$="1" THEN GO SUB 1250
1110 IF Z$="2" THEN GO SUB 1420
1120 IF Z$="3" THEN GO SUB 1550
1130 IF Z$="4" THEN GO SUB 1180
1140 IF Z$="5" THEN GO TO 1160
1150 CLS : GO TO 1000
1160 PRINT AT 10,10; FLASH 1; IN
K 2;"BANKER": INPUT "HAVE YOU EN
TERED ANY NEW DATA   YOU WANT TO
 SAVE? (Y/N)";Q$: IF Q$="Y" THEN
 SAVE "BANKER": BEEP 1,2: PRINT
"REWIND THEN ""ENTER"" TO VERIFY
": PAUSE 0: VERIFY "BANKER": PRI
NT "         PROGRAM VERIFIED"
1170 STOP
```

This is a standard menu module.

MODULE 2.3.2

```
1180 REM ************************
1190 REM VARIABLES
```

```
1200 REM **************************
1210 DIM A$(100,26): DIM A(100)
1220 DEF FN A$(X)=(STR$ (X+10000
.001))(2 TO 8)
1230 LET PAYMENTS=0
1240 RETURN
```

Commentary
Line 1210. A$ will be used to store the names and other information about the individual payments. A will store the actual amounts.

Line 1220. If you have followed the previous two programs you should have no difficulty in identifying the purpose of this function. In a single line, this function creates a standard format for any figure up to 9999.99 that it is let loose on. You may remember that in relation to Unifile, Module 2 we discussed the kinds of uses where a user-defined function resulted in a significant saving over a one or two line subroutine. This function, with its single argument, X, will be used to format two different variables, thus saving the use of two short subroutines. You might care, when you have familiarised yourself with its use in this program, to go back to the previous two and replace the short subroutines used to standardise the format of the figures.

Lines 1230. PAYMENTS is used to record the total number of items in the file.

MODULE 2.3.3

```
1250 REM **************************
1260 REM NEW REGULAR PAYMENT
1270 REM **************************
1280 PRINT AT 0,10; FLASH 1; INK
 2;"PAYMENTS"
1290 PRINT '"1) CREDIT / 2)DEBIT
? ";: INPUT CD: PRINT CD
1300 PRINT '"NAME OF PAYMENT? ";
: INPUT Q$: PRINT Q$
1310 PRINT '"AMOUNT? ";: INPUT Q
: PRINT Q
1320 PRINT '"MONTHS:e.g. 0104071
0 : ";: INPUT R$: PRINT R$
```

```
1330 PRINT '"DAY OF PAYMENT? ";:
 INPUT S: PRINT S
1340 INPUT "ARE THESE CORRECT? (
Y/N)";T$: IF T$="N" THEN CLS : G
O TO 1250
1350 LET PAYMENTS=PAYMENTS+1: FO
R J=PAYMENTS TO 2 STEP -1
1360 IF S<CODE A$(J-1,1) THEN LE
T A$(J)=A$(J-1): LET A(J)=A(J-1)
: NEXT J
1370 LET A$(J)="": LET A$(J,26)=
CHR$ CD: LET A$(J,14 TO 25)=Q$:
LET A(J)=Q
1380 IF CD=2 THEN LET A(J)=A(J)*
-1
1390: FOR I=1 TO LEN R$ STEP 2:
LET A$(J,1+VAL R$(I TO I+1))="1"
: NEXT I:
1400 LET A$(J,1)=CHR$ S
1410 RETURN
```

This module accepts the input of new items, including details of name, amount, months in which payment is made and the day of payment. The module also takes note of whether the item is a credit or a debit. If it is a debit, the amount is stored in a negative form.

Commentary

Lines 1350-1360. Starting with the last item in the file the module scans the items to find the first item that is smaller alphabetically than the item to be entered. This sorts the items into day of payment order, since the day of payment is recorded in the character code of the first character in each line in A$. Note that when inserting single items into an array it is always more efficient to start from the end of the list of items since each item can then be examined and, if necessary, shifted one place until the correct position is found. This eliminates the need for two separate loops, one to search through the file for the right position and another to shift the elements to make room for the new entry.

Lines 1370-1400. The amount is stored in A. The rest of the information is all stored in the same line of A$. The first character is used to store the day of payment: the next 12 are used to record the months in which the payment is made. Positions 14 to 25 are used for the name of the item. Position 26 records whether the item is a credit or a debit.

Testing Module 2.3.3
Run the program and call up the initialisation function. Now input a few items and then stop. Print out the contents of A$ and A and try to match them up with the description given in the commentary of this module.

MODULE 2.3.4

```
1550 REM ************************
1560 REM COMPILE STATEMENT
1570 REM ************************
1580 LET TOTAL=0
1590 PRINT AT 0,10; INK 2; FLASH
 1;"STATEMENT"
1600 PRINT ''"NUMBER OF MONTH FO
R STATEMENT:": INPUT Q: PRINT Q
1610 CLS : PRINT AT 0,10; INK 1;
"MONTH: ";Q
1620 FOR I=1 TO PAYMENTS
1630 IF A$(I,1+Q)<>"1" THEN GO T
O 1690
1640 IF A$(I,26)=CHR$ 1 THEN PAP
ER 6
1650 PRINT 'CODE A$(I,1);"*" AND
 A$(I,26)=CHR$ 1;TAB 3;":";A$(I,
14 TO 25);
1660 PRINT TAB 16;FN A$(ABS A(I)
);"_";: LET TOTAL=TOTAL+A(I): IF
 TOTAL<0 THEN INVERSE 1
1670 PRINT FN A$(ABS TOTAL): INV
ERSE 0
1680 PAPER 7
1690 NEXT I: INPUT """ENTER"" TO
 CONTINUE";Q$
1700 RETURN
```

This module accepts an input specifying a month and then prints out the accounts of all the payments and receipts during that month.

Commentary

Line 1630. Any item which does not have a 1 in the character position corresponding to the month specified is ignored.

Line 1640. PAPER colour is set to yellow for credit items.

Line 1650. Note the use of AND to print an asterisk next to the date of credit items.

Lines 1660-1670. FN A$ is applied to ABS A(I) and ABS TOTAL. Note the use of ABS here — the function would give a nonsense result if applied to a negative number due to the presence of the minus sign. The ABS could, of course, be included in the function.

Testing Module 2.3.4

Print out the accounts for the various months.

MODULE 2.3.5

```
1420 REM ************************
1430 REM DELETE PAYMENTS
1440 REM ************************
1450 FOR I=1 TO PAYMENTS
1460 CLS : IF CODE A$(I,26)=1 TH
EN PRINT ' PAPER 6;"CREDIT"
1470 IF C]DE A$(I,26)=2 THEN PRI
NT ' PAPER 6;"DEBIT"
1480 PRINT "PAYMENT:";A$(I,14 TO
 25)''"AMOUNT:";FN A$(ABS A(I))
1490>PRINT '"MONTHS:";: FOR J=1
TO 12: PRINT STR$ J AND A$(I,1+J
)="1";"/";: NEXT J
1500 PRINT ''"DAY OF PAYMENT:";C
ODE A$(I,1)
1510 PRINT PAPER 6;'"COMMANDS:"'
"1) ""DDD"" DELETE"'"2) ""ZZZ""
QUIT"'"3) ""ENTER"" FOR NEXT ITE
M."
1520 INPUT Q$: IF Q$="DDD" THEN
```

```
FOR J=I TO PAYMENTS: LET A$(J)=A
$(J+1): LET A(J)=A(J+1): NEXT J:
 LET PAYMENTS=PAYMENTS-1: RETURN

1530 IF Q$="" THEN NEXT I: RETUR
N
1540 RETURN
```

This module displays items from the file and gives the user the option of deleting them.

Commentary
Line 1520. Items are moved down the file to cover the one to be deleted. Note that this means the final item in the array is now duplicated since nothing was brought down to cover it. This is irrelevant since PAYMENTS is decreased by 1 and the position of what was the last item of the file becomes invisible to the program.

Testing Module 2.3.5
If the function works the program is now complete.

Summary
This is really a very simple program. It raises the interesting question of how far we should go in increasing a program's complexity to simplify its use. Sophisticated bank account programs often have facilities to register changes of year, frequency of payments, stop dates etc. In this program we have adopted the simple expedient of asking the user in which month the payment is to be made, thus eliminating the need to distinguish between one-off payments and a variety of different standing orders. I suspect that unless your financial transactions are extremely complex you will not want to go to the trouble of writing new program functions to cope with monthly payments without the user specifying the months. Watch out for over-complexity in your own programs; if you find yourself devoting 10 or 20 extra lines to functions which the human brain could do just as quickly before the data is input then you are wasting time and effort.

Going Further
1) The program has no facility to carry a balance forward from month to month. Have a go at adding one on.

2) The asterisk against the date of credit items is really there to make the item stand out when sent to the printer, which will not register the different paper colour. Duplicate the print statements in Module 4 with LPRINTs.

3) Could you combine the instruction to invert the printing of a negative number into the function FN A$?

CHAPTER 3

PAINTING A PICTURE — Spectrum graphics

In this chapter we examine some of the graphics capabilities of the Spectrum. To exhaust the Spectrum's graphics would be the work of a book in its own right and no attempt is made to do so here. We shall concentrate on bread and butter graphics which can be used to contribute to the effectiveness of a variety of programs. We shall leave aside such fascinating areas as three dimensional graphics, moving graphics and patterns created by mathematical functions. This is not to say that such areas are not important; it is simply that it would be impossible to do them justice here.

In the programs that follow we shall examine the possibilities opened up by the user-defined graphics capabilities and attempt to overcome some of the problems of creating and storing full screen designs.

The programs presented in this chapter are:

1) Characters — a program designed to allow you to create your own user-definable characters for use in other programs.
2) Dictionary — a method of storing the many user-defined graphics characters you will create.
3) Tangrams — a program which tackles the drawing of shapes using the DRAW command.
4) Artist — a program which allows you to draw full screen pictures using all the Spectrum's graphics characters, including user-defined ones and to store the resulting pictures together with their colour characteristics.
5) Designer — a program which allows you to define a design of up to 65536 * 65536 pixels across, to add and to delete, to examine the design at various scales and to rotate all or part of it on the screen.

3.1 Characters

Some of you may have written a character-defining program already. It is, however, a neat utility for those who have not and a simple introduction to some of the techniques we shall be using in other programs.

The program enables you to design, on a large scale, groups of up to four graphics characters, to delete existing graphics characters and to save on tape the character thus created.

If you are not familiar with the idea of user-defined graphics you should re-read chapter 14 of the Spectrum manual before trying to enter this program.

MODULE 3.1.1

```
1000 REM ************************
1010 REM MENU
1020 REM ************************
1030 PAPER 7: INK 0: CLS
1040 GO SUB 2400
1050 PRINT "          CHARACTERS
"
1060 PRINT '"FUNCTIONS AVAILABLE
:"
1070 PRINT '"1)INITIALISE"
1080 PRINT '"2)CREATE NEW CHARAC
TERS"
1090 PRINT '"3)SAVE CHARACTERS"
1100 PRINT '"4)DELETE CHARACTERS
"
1110 PRINT '"5)STOP"
1120 PRINT '"WHICH DO YOU REQUIR
E?"
1130 INPUT Z$
1140 CLS
1150 IF Z$="1" THEN GO SUB 1230
1160 IF Z$="2" THEN GO SUB 1290
1170 IF Z$="3" THEN GO SUB 2270
1180 IF Z$="4" THEN GO SUB 2040
1190 IF Z$="5" THEN STOP
1200 PAPER 7: CLS
1210 GO TO 1000
1220 STOP
```

This is a standard menu module.

MODULE 3.1.2

```
2400 REM ************************
2410 REM LOAD INITIAL CHARACTER
2420 REM ************************
2430 RESTORE
2440 FOR I=0 TO 7
2450 READ BYTE
2460 POKE USR CHR$ 144+I,BYTE
2470 NEXT I
2480 RETURN
2490 DATA 255,129,129,129,129,12
9,129,255
```

This module loads the character '□' into memory at the position occupied by 'A' in the user-defined graphics area. The character will be used in the course of the program.

Commentary
Lines 2440-2470. If you have re-read chapter 14 of the Spectrum manual you should have no difficulty understanding what is going on here. The numbers in the data statement represent binary values which, when stored in the user-defined character area will make up the character '□'. 255 translates into binary as 11111111 and 129 as 10000001. They are read one by one and placed into the memory. CHR$ 144 is 'A' in the user-defined area.

Testing Module 3.1.2
After entering and running this module, graphics 'A' should print the character '□'.

MODULE 3.1.3

```
1230 REM ************************
1240 REM VARIABLES
1250 REM ************************
1260 DIM Z(26,8)
1270 LET CHARACTERS=1
1280 RETURN
```

These are all the variables.

Commentary

Line 1260. The numbers which will be used to create the user-defined characters are stored in this array for ease of manipulation. Any deletions are accomplished first in the array and the array is then loaded into the memory.

MODULE 3.1.4

```
1290 REM ************************
1300 REM DRAW GRID
1310 REM ************************
1330 FOR I=2 TO 17
1340 FOR J=6 TO 21
1350 PRINT AT I,J;"A"
1360 NEXT J
1370 NEXT I
1380 FOR I=6 TO 21
1390 PRINT OVER 1; PAPER 5;AT 2,
I;" ";AT 9,I;" ";AT 10,I;" ";AT
17,I;" "
1400 NEXT I
1410 FOR I=2 TO 17
1420 PRINT OVER 1; PAPER 5;AT I,
6;" ";AT I,13;" ";AT I,14;" ";AT
 I,21;" "
1430 NEXT I
1440 PRINT AT 20,0;"5,6,7,8 TO M
OVEA1 TO INK INA0 TORUB OUTA9 TO
 REGISTER CHARACTERS"
```

This module draws 16*16 grid on which the user-defined characters will be built up. The grid is constructed out of the character defined in Module 2.

Commentary

Lines 1380-1430. There are four separate character squares. To help distinguish between them, their borders are shaded in blue, using the over characteristic to avoid rubbing out the grid.

Testing Module 3.1.4

The module should print a 16*16 grid with the borders of four 8*8 squares shaded in.

MODULE 3.1.5

```
1450 REM ************************
1460 REM FILL IN SQUARES
1470 REM ************************
1480 DIM A$(4,8,8)
1490 LET X=2: LET Y=6
1500 PRINT AT X,Y; PAPER 8; OVER
 1;"*": PAUSE 5
1510 PRINT AT X,Y; PAPER 8; OVER
 1;"*"
1520 LET T$=INKEY$
1530 IF T$="" THEN GO TO 1500
1540 BEEP .05,40
1550 LET X1=X-1-8*(X>9): LET Y1=
Y-5-8*(Y>13)
1560 LET XY=1+(Y>13)+2*(X>9)
1570 IF T$="0" THEN LET A$(XY,X1
,Y1)="A"
1580 IF T$="1" THEN LET A$(XY,X1
,Y1)="_"
1590 IF T$="9" THEN GO TO 1660
1600 PRINT PAPER 8;AT X,Y;"A";:
IF A$(XY,X1,Y1)="_" THEN PRINT P
APER 8;AT X,Y;"_"
1610 LET X=X+(T$="6")-(T$="7")
1620 LET X=X+(X<2)-(X>17)
1630 LET Y=Y-(T$="5")+(T$="8")
1640 LET Y=Y+(Y<6)-(Y>21)
1650 GO TO 1500
```

This module is the core of the program. Its purpose is to allow the user to move a flashing cursor around the grid, either inking in squares or erasing squares which are already inked in. When the character is defined to your satisfaction you can quit the module and examine that character in its correct size.

Commentary

Line 1480. It is far easier to manipulate the contents of an array than what is on the screen. Therefore when a square on the grid is to be inked in it is first recorded in the array A$ and it is A$ that is then printed on the screen. Note that the array A$ takes account in its dimensions of the fact that there are four separate character squares.

Line 1490. These are the co-ordinates of the top left-hand corner of the grid.

Lines 1500-1530. This routine prints a flashing cursor at position X,Y until a key is pressed. PAPER is set to 8 so that the shade of the square is left unchanged. Since the asterisk is printed OVER twice, it has no effect on the contents of the grid square.

Line 1540. The INKEY$ function does not activate the keyboard beep so this has to be replaced to show that a key has registered.

Lines 1550-1560. The X,Y co-ordinates are converted to co-ordinates in A$.

Lines 1610-1640. This is an extremely useful routine when it comes to moving a cursor around the screen under the control of the user. The use of the logical conditions in brackets alters the value of the X or the Y co-ordinate if one of the cursor arrow keys is pressed. Lines 1620 and 1640 check that the cursor has not moved outside the desired limits — which in other circumstances might be the edge of the screen. If the limits have been exceeded in any way the cursor is shunted back, again using a logical condition as a variable. These two checks will be found time and time again in programs which move something around the screen.

Testing Module 3.1.5

Run the program, initialise, then call up function 2 and move the flashing cursor around the grid, inking in and erasing at will.

MODULE 3.1.6

```
1660 REM ************************
1670 REM RECORD CHARACTERS
1680 REM ************************
1690 PAPER 7
1700 INPUT "Is the pattern satis
factory?     (ZZZ) TO QUIT";Q$
1710 IF Q$="ZZZ" THEN RETURN
1720 IF Q$="Y" THEN GO TO 1740
1730 PAPER 5: GO TO 1490
1740 INPUT "WHICH CELLS TO BE SA
VED? (ONE   DIGIT PER CELL, ANY
ORDER):";Q$
1750 LET CELLS=LEN Q$
1760 IF CHARACTERS+CELLS<=21 THE
N GO TO 1790
1770 PRINT AT 20,0;"NOT ENOUGH R
OOM."
1780 RETURN
1790 FOR I=1 TO CELLS
1800 FOR J=1 TO 8
1810 LET BYTE=0
1820 FOR H=1 TO 8
1830 IF A$(VAL Q$(I),J,H)="_" TH
EN LET BYTE=BYTE+2↑(8-H)
1840 NEXT H
1850 LET Z(CHARACTERS+I-1,J)=BYT
E
1860 NEXT J
1870 NEXT I
1890 LET CHARACTERS=CHARACTERS+C
ELLS
```

This module transfers the pattern created on the grid to the array Z in the form of a series of numbers which, when placed into the user-defined character memory area will reproduce the character just designed.

Commentary
Lines 1790-1870. Each line of A$ is treated, in effect, as an eight digit binary number, with each inked-in square representing a "1". The resulting number is placed into the relevant space in the array Z.

Testing Module 3.1.6
You may enter a character and check that sensible values have been entered into the array Z.

MODULE 3.1.7

```
1900 REM ************************
1910 REM ACTIVATE CHARACTERS
1920 REM ************************
1930 FOR I=1 TO 20
1940 FOR J=0 TO 7
1950 POKE USR CHR$ (144+I)+J,Z(I
,J+1)
1960 NEXT J
1970 NEXT I
1980 INPUT "Do you want to test
characters?";Q$
1990 IF Q$<>"Y" THEN RETURN
2000 PRINT "PRESS ANY KEY TO STA
RT, THEN    CHANGE TO GRAPHICS M
ODE."
2010 PAUSE 0
2020 CLS : INPUT Q$
2030 RETURN
```

The numbers stored in the array Z are placed into the user-defined character memory.

Commentary
Lines 1930-1970. This is a similar function to that carried out by module 2.

Line 2020. The string input in this line is merely an opportunity to input some characters and check the new user-defined characters that have been stored. The string serves no other purpose.

Testing Module 3.1.7

You are now in a position to enter up to 20 of your own characters and test that they have been properly stored in the memory.

MODULE 3.1.8

```
2040 REM ************************
2050 REM DELETE CHARACTERS
2060 REM ************************
2070 IF CHARACTERS=1 THEN RETURN

2080 FOR I=2 TO CHARACTERS
2090 PRINT CHR$ (143+I)
2100 PRINT ''"DO YOU WISH TO DEL
ETE THIS       CHARACTER? (Y/N)"
2110 INPUT Q$
2120 IF Q$="Y" THEN GO TO 2160
2130 CLS
2140 NEXT I
2150 RETURN
2160 FOR J=I-1 TO CHARACTERS-2
2170 FOR K=1 TO 8
2180 LET Z(J,K)=Z(J+1,K)
2190 NEXT K
2200 NEXT J
2210 FOR I=1 TO 8
2220 LET Z(J,I)=0
2230 NEXT I
2240 LET CHARACTERS=CHARACTERS-1
2250 GO SUB 1900
2260 RETURN
```

This module gives the user the option of deleting characters which have already been stored. Deletion is actually achieved by removing the relevant elements from the array Z and then re-entering the characters into memory.

Testing Module 3.1.8

Try deleting some characters and then examining the rest of the characters to make sure that they have not been corrupted in any way by the process.

MODULE 3.1.9

```
2270 REM ************************
2280 REM SAVE CHARACTERS
2290 REM ************************
2295 LET Y$="": FOR I=1 TO CHARA
CTERS-1: FOR J=1 TO 8: LET Y$=Y$
+CHR$ Z(I,J): NEXT J: NEXT I
2300 DIM X$(LEN Y$): LET X$=Y$
2305 FOR I=1 TO CHARACTERS-1
2310 PRINT CHR$ (144+I);" ";
2320 NEXT I
2330 PRINT '"WHAT NAME DO WANT T
O GIVE TO     THIS SET OF CHARACT
ERS?"
2340 INPUT N$: PRINT ''N$
2350 SAVE N$CODE USR "A",21*8
2355 SAVE N$ DATA X$()
2360 CLS : PRINT ''"NOW PLEASE R
EWIND TO BEGINNING, START TAPE,
THEN PRESS ANY KEY."
2370 PAUSE 0
2380 VERIFY N$CODE USR "A",21*8
2385 VERIFY N$ DATA X$()
2390 PRINT ''"CHARACTER SET VERI
FIED.": PAUSE 200: RETURN
```

The character set created by the user is given a name and saved on to cassette in two forms, one of which relates to the next program in this chapter.

Commentary
Line 2295. The values in Z are transferred, in the form of single character codes, to the string Y$. Since the Spectrum will not save such an undimensioned string, X$ is dimensioned to be the same size as Y$ and the contents of Y$ are transferred.

Lines 2300-2340. This section prints out the whole of the character set and invites the user to give it a name.

Line 2350. This line instructs the Spectrum to save the contents of its memory, starting at the beginning of the user-defined character area and including 168 bytes of memory i.e. all the memory devoted to user-defined characters.

Line 2355. The character set is also saved in the form of X$.

Line 2380. The character set stored on tape can be verified in the same way that a program can and it is wise to do so in case there was some fault in the recording of your hard-earned characters.

Testing Module 3.1.9
Create a set of characters and save it using this module. Make sure that you have saved the program, then disconnect momentarily to clear the contents of the memory. Now enter LOAD N$ — using whatever name you gave in N$ — CODE USR'A', 21*8 and then replay what you have saved. When loading is complete you should discover that the new characters have returned. If so, the program is correctly entered and ready for use.

Summary
Apart from its usefulness in creating characters for use in other programs, in this program you have encountered a number of techniques you will come back to time and time again in graphics programs. These include the flashing cursor, the use of the cursor keys to move a character on the screen, the use of logical conditions to set boundaries for that movement and the use of arrays to simulate the screen.

Going Further
1) Have a go at increasing the number of characters that can be defined in one block from four to six.
2) Make the program print the developing characters' proper size alongside the grid as they are being constructed.

3.2 Dictionary
This short program greatly increases the usefulness of the character generator by allowing the user to create a dictionary of all the user-defined characters previously created. The user can then draw on the whole of this reserve to create new combinations of characters in character sets.

MODULE 3.2.1

```
1000 REM ************************
1010 REM MENU
1020 REM ************************
1030 INK 0: PAPER 7: CLS : PRINT
 "        CHARACTER DICTIONARY"
1040 PRINT '"1) INITIALISE"
1050 PRINT '"2) LOAD NEW CHARACT
ERS"
1060 PRINT '"3) CREATE NEW SET"
1070 PRINT '"4) SAVE SET OF CHAR
ACTERS"
1080 PRINT '"5) STOP"
1090 INPUT Z$: CLS
1100 IF Z$="1" THEN GO SUB 1180
1110 IF Z$="2" THEN GO SUB 1430
1120 IF Z$="3" THEN GO SUB 1220
1130 IF Z$="4" THEN GO SUB 1360
1140 IF Z$="5" THEN GO TO 1160
1150 GO TO 1030
1160 INPUT "DO YOU WISH TO RE-RE
CORD? (Y/N)";Q$: IF Q$="Y" THEN
SAVE "DICTIONARY": BEEP 1,40: PR
INT AT 10,0;"REWIND, THEN ANY KE
Y TO VERIFY.": PAUSE 0: VERIFY "
DICTIONARY": PRINT '"PROGRAM VER
IFIED"
1170 STOP
```

A standard menu module.

MODULE 3.2.2

```
1180 REM ************************
1190 REM INITIALISE
1200 REM ************************
1210 LET P$="": RETURN
```

The initialisation module.

Commentary
Line 1210. This string is used to store the values which will be poked into the user-defined memory area.

MODULE 3.2.3

```
1430 REM ************************
1440 REM LOAD NEW CHARACTERS
1450 REM ************************
1460 INPUT "NAME OF CHARACTER SE
T? ";N$
1470 LOAD N$CODE USR "A",168: LO
AD N$ DATA T$()
1480 FOR I=0 TO 20: PRINT CHR$ (
144+I);" ";: NEXT I
1490 INPUT "DO YOU WANT THIS SET
? (Y/N)";Q$: IF Q$="N" THEN RETU
RN
1500 LET P$=P$+T$: RETURN
```

This module loads from tape the character sets created by the previous program and adds them to the dictionary.

Testing Module 3.2.3
With this module in place you should be able to load character sets from tape. P$ should be eight times the number of characters loaded.

MODULE 3.2.4

```
1220 REM ************************
1230 REM PRINTCHARACTERS
1240 REM ************************
1250 FOR I=0 TO 167: POKE USR "A
"+I,0: NEXT I
```

```
1260 LET C$=""
1270 FOR I=1 TO LEN P$/160+1: PR
INT AT 0,10;"PAGE ";I: FOR J=1 T
O 20: FOR K=1 TO 8
1280 IF 160*(I-1)+8*(J-1)+K>LEN
P$ THEN GO TO 1310
1290 POKE USR "A"+(K-1),CODE P$(
160*(I-1)+8*(J-1)+K): NEXT K
1300 PRINT 20*(I-1)+J;" ";CHR$ 1
44: NEXT J
1310 INPUT "CHAR.NO. N=NEXT PAGE
 ZZZ=QUIT";N$: IF N$="N" THEN GO
 TO 1350
1315 IF N$="ZZZ" THEN RETURN
1320 LET C$=C$+P$(8*(VAL N$-1)+1
 TO 8*VAL N$): IF LEN C$=168 THE
N PRINT AT 21,0;"CHARACTER SET F
ULL": PAUSE 100: RETURN
1330 GO TO 1310
1350 CLS : NEXT I: RETURN
```

This module prints out the dictionary and invites the user to specify which characters are to be included in the new character set which is being created.

Commentary

Line 1250. Any existing user-defined characters are cleared.

Lines 1270-1350. Three loops are involved here. The I loop prints out pages of 20 characters; the J loop prints the individual characters which make up the pages and the K loop pokes the eight values which make up each individual character. Each character is poked into the position normally occupied by A in the user-defined graphics area and then printed.

Testing Module 3.2.4

You should now be able to make up new character sets out of the material provided by the previous program.

Module 3.2.5

```
1360 REM ************************
1370 REM PLACE IN MEMORY
```

```
1380 REM ************************
1390 FOR I=1 TO LEN C$: POKE USR
 "A"+I-1,CODE C$(I): NEXT I
1400 FOR I=0 TO 20: PRINT CHR$ (
144+I): NEXT I
1410 INPUT "NAME FOR CHARACTER S
ET?";N$: SAVE N$CODE USR "A",168
1420 INPUT "REWIND THEN ENTER TO
 VERIFY.";Q$: VERIFY N$CODE USR
"A",168: PRINT AT 21,0;"CHARACTE
R SET VERIFIED.": PAUSE 200: RET
URN
```

This module displays the character set, invites the user to give it a name and then stores it as a block of code to be picked up by other programs as desired.

Testing Module 3.2.5
You should now be able to store your character sets, disconnect the Spectrum and re-load the new character set. Do not forget to save the program first.

3.3 Tangrams

This is a program that simply begs to be built up according to your own tastes. It allows the user to play the ancient Chinese shape-making game of Tangrams, with its two small triangles, one medium and two large, coupled with a square and a parallelogram. More than that, however, the program is an indication of how both regular and irregular geometric shapes can be simply drawn in a variety of positions or orientations, without recourse to complex mathematics, although it is easier if you know some maths.

MODULE 3.3.1

```
1000 REM ************************
1010 REM VARIABLES
1020 REM ************************
1030 DEF FN A()=SIDE*COS (A*PI/4
)
1040 DEF FN B()=SIDE*SIN (A*PI/4
)
1050 LET X=100: LET Y=100
```

```
1060 INPUT "CLEAR SCREEN? (Y/N)
";Q$: PAPER 6: INK 1: IF Q$="Y"
THEN CLS
1070 LET L$="MOVE WITH CURSOR AR
ROWS OR ""9"""
1080 LET K$="""0"" TO ABANDON SH
APE                "
1090 LET J$="""1"" TO RECORD SCR
EEN OR QUIT.       "
1100 DIM O$(32)
```

Note that there is no menu to this program. All the instructions are given at the bottom of the screen during the course of the program. This module sets up the necessary variables.

Commentary

Lines 1030-1040. These two simple functions are used for the purpose of determining the end points of lines to be drawn. In order to draw a line using the two functions it is only necessary to know the starting point, the angle and the length of the line. Given those, the functions will define two co-ordinates which will be sufficient to allow the DRAW command to be used. A glance at pages 68 and 69 of the Spectrum manual will show how the COS and SIN functions can be used to accomplish this. Note that the functions can handle only those angles which can be expressed in units of PI-4 radians or 1/8th of a circle. If you would like greater flexibility a larger divisor could be inserted, such as 180 which would result in units of one degree.

Line 1050. These are the starting points from which any drawing will be done.

MODULE 3.3.2

```
1650 REM ************************
1660 REM MOVING PIXEL
1670 REM ************************
1680 PRINT AT 20,0;L$'J$
1690 OVER 1: FOR I=1 TO 2: PLOT
BRIGHT 1 AND I=1;X,Y: PLOT X,Y+1
: PLOT X,Y+2: PAUSE 1+2*(I=1): N
EXT I: OVER 0: PLOT INVERSE 1; O
VER 1;X,Y
```

```
1700 LET T$=INKEY$: IF T$="" THE
N GO TO 1690
1710 IF T$="9" THEN RETURN
1720 IF T$="1" THEN GO TO 1330
1730 IF T$>"9" OR T$<"5" THEN GO
 TO 1690
1740 LET X=X+(T$="8")-(T$="5"):
LET X=X-(X>245)+(X<5)
1750 LET Y=Y+(T$="7")-(T$="6"):
LET Y=Y+(Y<20)-(Y>170)
1760 GO TO 1690
```

This module prints a small flashing cursor in the position at which any shape drawn will start and allows the user to move the cursor without altering the contents of the screen. The method is similar to the cursor module in the first program of this chapter but here only three pixels are involved.

Commentary
Line 1690. Note the use of the logical condition to set the BRIGHT characteristic. PLOT INVERSE 1; OVER 1 is a way of moving the plot position without plotting a point. It is used because at the end of the loop the plot position has moved to XY + 2. The character position is set to BRIGHT in order to make it easier to see the small cursor.

Lines 1740-1750. These lines are exactly parallel to those used in the last program to move the cursor and set limits to its movement.

Testing Module 3.3.2
You should be able to run the program and move the tiny cursor around the screen.

MODULE 3.3.3

```
1110 REM ***********************
1120 REM SELECT SHAPE
1130 REM ***********************
1140 GO SUB 1650: PRINT AT 20,0;
O$;K$: LET SUPP=3
1150 INPUT "1:T 2:P 3:S 4:C ";SH
APE: IF SHAPE=0 THEN GO TO 1110
```

```
1160 IF SHAPE=4 THEN GO SUB 1410
 : GO TO 1110
1170 IF SHAPE=2 THEN INPUT "TYPE
 1 OR 2 ";SUPP: IF SUPP=0 THEN G
O TO 1110
1180 IF SHAPE=1 THEN INPUT "SIZE
 (1,2,3) ";SIZE: IF SIZE=0 THEN
GO TO 1110
1190 INPUT "ORIENTATION ";O: LET
 O=3-O: LET A=O: IF O=3 THEN GO
TO 1110
1200 INPUT "CORNER? ";C1: IF C1=
0 THEN GO TO 1110
1210 LET LONG=36: IF SHAPE=1 THE
N LET LONG=36*((SQR 2)^SIZE)-.5
1220 LET SHORT=LONG/SQR 2
1230 INPUT "DRAW:1 ERASE:2 ";DRA
W: OVER 1
1240 IF SHAPE=1 THEN GO SUB 1470
1250 IF SHAPE=2 THEN GO SUB 1520
1260 IF SHAPE=3 THEN GO SUB 1570
1270 IF DRAW=1 THEN INPUT "CONFI
RM SHAPE? (Y/N) ";Q$: LET A=O: O
VER (Q$="N"): PLOT INVERSE 1; OV
ER 1;X,Y
1280 IF DRAW<>1 THEN OVER 0: GO
TO 1110
1290 IF SHAPE=1 THEN GO SUB 1470
1300 IF SHAPE=2 THEN GO SUB 1520
1310 IF SHAPE=3 THEN GO SUB 1570
1320 OVER 0: GO TO 1110
```

This module accepts the information necessary to print a shape.

Commentary

Line 1150. The program as it stands is capable of drawing four basic shapes: triangles, parallelograms, squares and circles. In any input in this module '0' will result in a return to the flashing cursor.

Line 1170. Parallelograms are not symmetrical, so the program has to be told which way round to print one. SUPP records which one is specified.

Line 1180. Three sizes of triangle are available; they are symmetrical, right angled and each is twice the area of the next smallest.

Line 1190. For each shape a key corner is chosen as shown in the illustration. Following on clockwise from this corner is the key side and it is the angle of this side which is input here.

Line 1200. Having determined the angle of the key side it only remains to say which of the shape's corners will fall on the spot which was marked by the cursor. Corners are numbered from the key corner. All of this may sound highly complicated but in use it will become obvious.

Line 1210. The long sides of the small triangles and of the parallelograms are 36 pixels long, a figure chosen arbitrarily. The short sides are accordingly 36/SQR 2 pixels long — have a word with Pythagoras if you disagree. The long sides of the larger triangles increase in multiples of two.

Lines 1230-1320. This section calls up the routines which draw the shapes, except the circle. Each routine is called twice. On the first occasion the shape is drawn OVER what is already there. This results in any lines touched being deleted or shared by the new shape. This still allows the user to see whether the shape is in the right position. If the user confirms the shape it is drawn again with OVER set at zero, thus making good any gaps. If the figure is not confirmed it is drawn OVER again and thus erased. The user can also erase a figure with a corner at the point marked by the cursor — this will result in the permanent loss of any shared lines.

Testing Module 3.3.3
No shapes can yet be drawn but the program should now accept all the characteristics specified above.

MODULE 3.3.4

```
1410 REM ************************
1420 REM CIRCLE
1430 REM ************************
1440 INPUT "RADIUS? ";R: IF R=0
THEN RETURN
1450 CIRCLE OVER 1;X,Y,R
1460 INPUT "CONFIRM CIRCLE? (Y/N
) ";Q$: CIRCLE OVER (Q$="N");X,Y
,R: RETURN
```

This module allows the user to set a radius and draw a circle with its origins at the point marked by the cursor, with the option to delete it again.

Testing Module 3.3.4
You should be able to move the cursor to a chosen spot and draw a circle around that spot.

MODULE 3.3.5

```
1610 REM ***********************
1620 REM DRAW SHAPE
1630 REM ***********************
1640  DRAW FN A(),FN B(): RETURN
```

This module lays down the end point of a line which will comprise one end of a shape. The two functions have been explained earlier.

MODULE 3.3.6

```
1470 REM ***********************
1480 REM TRIANGLES
1490 REM ***********************
1500 LET A$="036": FOR I=0 TO 2:
 LET I1=C1+I-3*((I+C1)>3): LET S
IDE=SHORT: IF I1=2 THEN LET SIDE
=LONG
1510 LET A=0-VAL A$(I1): GO SUB
1610: NEXT I: RETURN
```

This module, when used with the last module, draws triangles.

Commentary
Lines 1500-1510. The method employed here is simple. For each figure a string is created. The individual characters of the string record how many 45 degree units each line has to be turned clockwise in relation to the key side. Thus the key side is clearly at zero units to itself. In the case of a triangle the next side is at an angle of 135 degrees, or three units, to the key side. The simple loop in these

two lines combines the angle input for the key side with each of the characters in the string in turn to determine the angle each side. The variable I1 ensures that if the loop does not start at 1, it reduces to 1 when it passes 3. Note the split in the loop caused by the presence of an If statement.

Testing Module 3.3.6
You should now be able to specify and draw triangles.

MODULE 3.3.7

```
1520 REM ************************
1530 REM PARALLELOGRAM
1540 REM ************************
1550 LET A$="0145": FOR I=0 TO 3
: LET I1=C1+I-4*(I+C1)>4): LET
SIDE=LONG: IF I1=2 OR I1=4 THEN
LET SIDE=SHORT
1560 LET A=O-VAL A$(I1)+2*VAL A$
(I1)*(SUPP=2): GO SUB 1610: NEXT
 I: RETURN
```

This is similar to Module 6 except that it draws a parallelogram. Note how SUPP is used to determine which type of parallelogram is drawn.

MODULE 3.3.8

```
1570 REM ************************
1580 REM SQUARE
1590 REM ************************
1600 LET SIDE=LONG: FOR I=0 TO 3
: LET A=O-2*I: GO SUB 1610: NEXT
 I: RETURN
```

This method prints out a square by a different method to that employed by the previous two. In this case the angle of the key side is simply incremented regularly and a side drawn. This method would work for any regular figure and it would be a simple task to allow the user to specify the number of sides, the change in angle for each side being 2Pi/X, where X is the number of sides.

Testing Module 3.3.8
All the program's shape-drawing capabilities should now be available.

MODULE 3.3.9

```
1330 REM ************************
1340 REM SAVE PATTERN
1350 REM ************************
1360 INPUT "DO YOU WANT TO QUIT?
 (Y/N)";Q$: IF Q$="Y" THEN STOP
1370 INPUT "NAME OF PATTERN:";N$
1380 PRINT AT 20,0;"RESTART PROG
RAM WITH GO TO 1
                                "
1390 SAVE N$SCREEN$
1400 STOP
```

This module allows the pattern created to be saved on to cassette for later use.

Commentary
Line 1390. This command saves on to tape the contents of 6912 memory locations which are used to store the contents of the screen. When dealing with graphics where individual pixels have been defined rather than characters, it is the only practical method of storage.

Testing Module 3.3.9
Create a pattern and save it on tape. Clear the screen and recall the pattern by entering LOAD "Name" SCREEN$ and replaying the tape. The picture should be rebuilt gradually. By starting the program again with GOTO 1 you should be able to add to the picture as if it had never been absent.

Summary
If you are interested in producing shapes simply and under your own control, the techniques unfolded in this chapter will be of great use to you. With them you can tackle both regular and irregular straight-edged figures. The technique of storing relative angles in a short string can be used to define quite complex perimeters which would be practically impossible to analyse mathematically. The modules to draw such figures would, as the program shows, be short and require few variables, so that they are practical candidates for addition to other programs which could benefit from the drawing of some shapes.

Going Further
1) In the module which draws circles, there is no provision to erase a circle which has already been drawn. Can you add one?
2) Try adding a module which would draw an octagon, using the same style as the module which draws squares.
3) Alter the program so that it can draw at any angle rather than being limited to 45 degree units.

3.4 Artist
This program, or one like it, is an important part of the process of building up a library of programs. If you are going to have programs which use pictures as part of their output, then you must be able to create pictures simply and store them.

The intention of any program like this is to enhance the Spectrum's capabilities by allowing the cursor to be moved over the whole screen and enabling graphics characters to be printed at any position on the screen with the minimum amount of key-pressing. Lastly it would be desirable in any such program if the designs created could be stored more economically than by using the SCREEN$ function, which requires nearly 7,000 bytes of memory and is quite slow to load. Since we shall not be using SCREEN$, however, we shall be able to use only whole graphics characters, including user-defined characters. The program will behave as if designs created with DRAW, CIRCLE or PLOT commands are not there.

Note: If you intend to use user-defined graphics in any design to be stored, any subsequent program which picks up the design must have been loaded with the same characters.

MODULE 3.4.1

```
1000 REM ****************************
1010 REM VARIABLES
1020 REM ****************************
1030 DIM B$(2,30): FOR I=1 TO 30
: LET B$(1,I)="8": LET B$(2,I)=C
HR$ 0: NEXT I
1040 DIM A$(3,20,30): FOR I=1 TO
 20: LET A$(2,I)=B$(1): LET A$(3
,I)=B$(2): NEXT I
1050 LET X=1: LET Y=1
1060 LET T=4
1070 DIM O$(32)
```

```
1080 PAPER 7: INK 0: CLS
1090 LET MODE=1: DIM L$(2,20): L
ET L$(1)="(MODE 1)": LET L$(2)="
(MODE 2)"
1100 GO SUB 1320
```

Commentary
Line 1030. This line creates a temporary expedient, B$, which is used to speed up the process of loading the main array, A$.

Line 1040. The array A$ will ultimately be used to store three sets of information:

a) The actual characters on the screen.
b) The colour characteristics of each of the characters.
c) Whether the character is to be printed in inverse video.

The second part of the array is loaded with '8's because the code of this character, 56, is the same as that of an attribute byte laying down an ink of 0 and a paper of 7. For a further explanation of the ATTR codes which determine colour characteristics, see page 116 of the Spectrum manual. The third section of the array is filled with CHR$ 0 to signify that there are no inverted characters.

Line 1060. This variable records the direction in which the cursor will move, expressed in 1/8th segments of a circle, starting with 1 for straight up.

Line 1090. MODE is the variable used to record whether normal or inverse characters will be printed.

MODULE 3.4.2

```
1320 REM ***********************
1325 REM ACCEPT CHARACTERS
1330 REM ***********************
1340 PRINT INK 0; PAPER 7;AT 0,0
;L$(MODE);AT 21,0;"SPACE W=ATTR
X=ST Y=REC Z=MO  ";AT 0,21;"DIRE
CTION=";T
1350 PRINT INK 0; PAPER 7; OVER
1;AT X,Y;"*": PAUSE 3: PRINT INK
 0; PAPER 7; OVER 1;AT X,Y;"*"
1360 LET T$=INKEY$
```

```
1370 IF T$="" THEN GO TO 1350
1380 BEEP .05,12
1390 IF CODE T$>32 AND CODE T$<4
1 THEN LET T=CODE T$-32: GO TO 1
340
1400 IF CODE T$=64 THEN LET T=2:
 GO TO 1340
1410 IF T$="W" THEN GO SUB 1170:
 GO TO 1320
1420 IF T$="X" THEN STOP
1430 IF T$="Y" THEN GO SUB 1600:
 GO TO 1320
1440 IF T$="Z" THEN LET MODE=MOD
E+1: LET MODE=MODE-2*(MODE>2): G
O TO 1320
1450 IF T$=" " THEN POKE (22528+
32*X+Y),CODE A$(2,X,Y): GO SUB 1
540: GO TO 1340
1460 IF T$="0" THEN PRINT AT X,Y
;" ": LET A$(1,X,Y)=" ": LET A$(
2,X,Y)=CHR$ ATTR (X,Y): GO SUB 1
540: GO TO 1340

1470 IF MODE<>1 THEN GO TO 1510
1480 IF CODE T$>=49 AND CODE T$<
=56 THEN LET T$=CHR$ (CODE T$+80
): LET T$=CHR$ (CODE T$-8*(CODE
T$=136)): GO SUB 1110: LET A$(3,
X,Y)=CHR$ 0: GO SUB 1540: GO TO
1350
1490 IF CODE T$>=65 AND CODE T$<
=85 THEN LET T$=CHR$ (79+CODE T$
): LET A$(3,X,Y)=CHR$ 0: GO SUB
1110: GO SUB 1540: GO TO 1350
1500 IF MODE<>2 THEN GO TO 1350
1510 IF CODE T$>=49 AND CODE T$<
=56 THEN LET T$=CHR$ (191-CODE T
$): LET T$=CHR$ (CODE T$+8*(CODE
 T$=135)): LET A$(3,X,Y)=CHR$ 0:
 GO SUB 1110: GO SUB 1540: GO TO
 1350
```

```
1520 IF CODE T$>=65 AND CODE T$<
=85 THEN LET T$=CHR$ (79+CODE T$
): LET A$(3,X,Y)=CHR$ 1: GO SUB
1110: GO SUB 1540: GO TO 1350
1530 GO TO 1320
```

This module allocates work among the modules which make up the rest of the program and translates characters input into graphics characters in accordance with the mode currently in force.

Commentary

Lines 1390-1400. The user is not required to specify direction or move the cursor each time a character is entered. It moves automatically in one of eight directions. The direction is set by holding down the Symbol Shift key and pressing one of the keys from 1 to 8.

Line 1450. If the user wishes to move the cursor past a character without altering the colour characteristics to those currently in force, this can be done by simply entering a space. The original colour characteristics of that character position, which were stored in the second part of A$, are poked back into the attributes byte corresponding to the character space. You will, I hope, have already noted that printing the cursor twice using OVER ensures that the actual character in the character space will be unchanged anyway.

Line 1460. Input of zero deletes whatever is in the character square.

Lines 1480-1520. According to the mode set, the actual code of the character on the key depressed is translated into the code of the graphics character desired. The routine which prints the character is then called up and the cursor moved. Note that the inverse characters associated with keys 1-8 are not really inverse. They are simply another set of characters taken from the character set. The inverse user-defined characters are really inverse; that is to say that they are printed with paper and ink reversed. For these, a marker is placed into the third area of A$.

Testing Module 3.4.2

With this module installed you should see the flashing cursor, the shorthand instructions at the bottom of the screen and the cursor direction in the top right-hand corner. You should be able to change the direction by holding down Symbol Shift and pressing one of the keys from 1-8. You should be able to change the mode by pressing the Z key. You cannot yet enter any characters.

MODULE 3.4.3

```
1540 REM ***************************
1550 REM MOVE INCREMENT
1560 REM ***************************
1570 LET X=X+(T=4)+(T=5)+(T=6)-(
T=8)-(T=1)-(T=2): LET X=X+(X<1)-
(X>20)
1580 LET Y=Y-(T=6)-(T=7)-(T=8)+(
T=2)+(T=3)+(T=4): LET Y=Y+(Y<1)-
(Y>30)
1590 RETURN
```

This is a standard cursor move module.

Testing Module 3.4.3
You should now be able to move the cursor in the chosen direction by pressing the space or zero keys.

MODULE 3.4.4

```
1110 REM ***************************
1120 REM ORDINARY GRAPHICS
1130 REM ***************************
1140 LET A$(1,X,Y)=T$
1150 PRINT INVERSE (CODE A$(3,X,
Y)=1);AT X,Y;T$
1160 LET A$(2,X,Y)=CHR$ ATTR (X,
Y): RETURN
```

This module prints the desired character in the cursor position.

Commentary
Line 1140. The character to be printed is placed in the equivalent position in the first part of A$.

Line 1150. The character is printed in inverse if there is a marker in the third section of A$.

Line 1160. The colour characteristics are picked up using the ATTR function and stored in the second area of A$.

Testing Module 3.4.4
You should now be able to print any graphics characters at any position within the 20*30 grid. You cannot set colour characteristics until the next module is entered.

MODULE 3.4.5

```
1170 REM ************************
1180 REM ATTRIBUTES
1190 REM ************************
1200 PRINT AT 0,0;"ATTRIBUTES
"
1210 DIM Q(4)
1220 FOR I=1 TO 4
1230 INPUT CHR$ (216+I);Q(I)
1240 IF Q(I)>9 THEN GO TO 1230
1250 IF I=1 THEN INK Q(I)
1260 IF I=2 THEN PAPER Q(I)
1270 IF I>2 AND Q(I)>1 THEN GO T
O 1230
1280 IF I=3 THEN FLASH Q(I)
1290 IF I=4 THEN BRIGHT Q(I)
1300 NEXT I
1310 RETURN
```

This simple module requests four inputs which set the characteristics for INK, PAPER, FLASH and BRIGHT.

Testing Module 3.4.5
You should now be able to vary the colour characteristics at various points on the screen.

MODULE 3.4.6

```
1600 REM ***************************
1610 REM CREATE PACKED STRING
1620 REM ***************************
1630 PRINT INK 0; PAPER 7;AT 21,0;"RECORDING
     "; INVERSE 0
1640 LET S$="": LET SPACE=0: LET IND=1
1650 FOR I=1 TO 20: FOR J=1 TO 30
1660 PRINT INK 0;AT I,0;"_"
1670 IF A$(1,I,J)=" " THEN LET SPACE=SPACE+1: LET IND=1: GO TO 1700
1680 IF IND=1 THEN LET S$=S$+CHR$ 255+CHR$ SPACE: LET IND=0: LET SPACE=0
1690 LET S$=S$+A$(1,I,J)+A$(2,I,J)+A$(3,I,J)
1700 NEXT J
1710 IF IND=1 THEN LET S$=S$+CHR$ 255+CHR$ SPACE
1720 LET IND=1: LET SPACE=0
1730 NEXT I
1740 BEEP 1,2
```

This module creates a packed string; that is, a string with all the spaces removed, out of the design stored in A$. The number of spaces removed is stored in single character indicators within the string.

Commentary

Line 1670. If the loop encounters a space it registers this in the variable SPACE and sets the indicator IND. This process continues until a non-space character is encountered.

Line 1680. Having encountered a character that is not a space, a marker is added to the string (CHR$ 255 or COPY) followed by a single character recording the number of spaces that have been missed out.

Line 1690. The three relevant bytes from the three areas of A$ are added to the packed string.

Line 1710. The end of each line in A$ is marked by COPY followed by the number of any spaces which preceded the end of the line.

MODULE 3.4.7

```
1750 REM ************************
1760 REM PRINT PACKED STRING
1770 REM ************************
1780 PAPER 7: CLS : PRINT AT 1,1
;: LET S=0: LET C=1
1790 IF S$(C)=CHR$ 255 THEN LET
C=C+1: IF S$(C)<>CHR$ 0 THEN PRI
NT O$( TO CODE S$(C));: LET S=S+
CODE S$(C): PRINT "  " AND S/30=
INT (S/30);: LET C=C+1: IF C<=LE
N S$ THEN GO TO 1790
1800 IF C>LEN S$ THEN GO TO 1840
1810 IF S$(C)=CHR$ 0 THEN LET C=
C+1
1820 LET S=S+1: INVERSE CODE S$(
C+2): PRINT S$(C);: POKE (23296-
32*(PEEK 23689)-PEEK 23688+32),C
ODE S$(C+1): INVERSE 0: IF S/30=
INT (S/30) THEN PRINT "  ";
1830 LET C=C+3: IF C<=LEN S$ THE
N GO TO 1790
1840 INPUT INK 0; PAPER 7;"SAVE
IT? (Y/N)";Q$
1850 IF Q$<>"Y" THEN RETURN
1860 INPUT "PLEASE GIVE THE PICT
URE A NAME:";N$
1870 DIM P$(LEN S$): LET P$=S$
1880 SAVE N$ DATA P$()
1890 INPUT "REWIND TAPE, PRESS "
"ENTER""    THEN START TAPE TO V
ERIFY";Q$
1900 VERIFY N$ DATA P$()
1910 PRINT AT 21,0;"PICTURE VERI
```

```
FIED:": STOP
1920 INPUT T$: PRINT CODE T$: GO
 TO 1920
```

This module re-prints the packed string for inspection and saves it on request.

Commentary
Line 1790. This line examines the packed string for the special marker, COPY, which indicates that the next character records a number of spaces that have been removed. When a marker is found, the correct number of spaces is inserted. Note that two spaces have to be printed at the end of each line to take account of the fact that the original grid was only 30 characters wide.

Line 1820. If the character in position C is not an indicator it is printed, with inverse set if the next but one character, C + 2, is CHR$ 1. The colour characteristics are then set by POKEing the value of character C + 1 into the attributes area.

Line 1830. The counter moves on three spaces since each character requires three spaces in the packed string.

Lines 1840-1910. If the user wishes to save the design as stored in the packed string, the design is first given a name. Note that the Spectrum will not properly save strings which have not been dimensioned, so that we have to create a new string, P$, of the same length as the packed string.

Once saved the design can be picked up from tape by another program and reprinted by a routine such as that in lines 1780-1830. See also Module 4.2.5.

Summary
Using this suite of three programs you have a set of tools which will enable you to enhance many of your programs and undertake many applications which would not be possible without any effective graphics tools.

In designing your own graphics you may well find that some sheets of squared paper are a help in mapping out your intentions before you sit down at the keyboard; you will find that you save a lot of time. If you can find designs of the right size it can also be helpful to trace them out on to transparent plastic and then stick the transparent sheet over the TV screen. Then simply follow the pattern you have traced.

Going Further

1) A full screen design stored by this program can still require up to 180 characters. If you need the inverse characteristics in your designs, this can be reduced by 1/3. If you only require single colour designs, you only need a single character space to record each character of the design. In one of the applications in the chapter on educational uses it is assumed that you have modified the packed string modules so that they store and reproduce only the characters and not the attributes.

2) Design a dictionary for your designs, if you have the memory. i.e. a program that will store a fair number of designs and display them on demand or in sequence.

3) Two further modes can be added, one to accept normal keyboard letters and numbers, the other to accept their inverse. The problem is that commands cannot be given unless you are going to start excluding keys. Using ENTER (CHR$ 13) as the command to change mode you can use the two modes although not issue commands. Can you adapt the program for this?

3.5 Designer

I have a special fondness for this program because the ideas on which it is based were not my own: they were taken from an excellent book, "The Principles of Interactive Computer Graphics" by William M Newman and Robert F Sproull. The reason I say fondness is that the program serves as a reminder to me of how much there is always to learn about the principles of programming and how many fields lie waiting to be opened up for no more cost than the price of a few books. Based on two simple procedures taken from the book, this program allows you to define a design of up to 65536 * 65536 pixels across, to add and to delete, to examine the design at various scales and to rotate all or part of it on the screen. Once its use is mastered it is capable of being used in a variety of applications where it is desirable to be able to change and manipulate designs quickly and easily.

MODULE 3.5.1

```
1000 REM ************************
1010 REM MENU
1020 REM ************************
1030 INK 0: PAPER 6: CLS : PRINT
 PAPER 2; INK 7;AT 1,10;"DESIGNE
R"
1040 PRINT '"COMMANDS AVAILABLE:
"
1050 PRINT "     1)INITIIALISE DI
SPLAY"
1060 PRINT "     2)ADD NEW LINES"
```

```
1070 PRINT "    3)SCALE/ROTATE"
1080 PRINT "    4)DELETE LINES"
1090 PRINT "    5)STOP"
1100 INPUT Z$: CLS
1110 IF Z$="1" THEN GO SUB 1190
1120 IF Z$="2" THEN GO SUB 1530
1130 IF Z$="3" THEN LET SEARCH=0
: GO SUB 1780
1140 IF Z$="4" THEN LET SEARCH=1
: GO SUB 1780
1150 IF Z$="5" THEN GO TO 1170
1160 CLS : GO TO 1000
1170 INPUT "DO YOU WISH TO SAVE
THIS DESIGN? ";Q$: IF Q$="Y" THE
N SAVE "DESIGNER": PRINT "REWIND
,THEN ANY KEY TO VERIFY": PAUSE
0: VERIFY "DESIGNER": PRINT "VER
IFIED"
1180 STOP
```

This is a standard menu module.

MODULE 3.5.2

```
1190 REM ************************
1200 REM INITIALISE
1210 REM ***********************
1220 LET LEFT=0: LET BOTTOM=0: L
ET TOP=167: LET RIGHT=255
1230 LET A$=""
1240 DEF FN A( )=256*CODE (A$(I1)
)+CODE A$(I1+1)
1250 DEF FN A$( )=CHR$ INT (TX1/2
56)+CHR$ (TX1-256*INT (TX1/256))
+CHR INT (TY1/256)+CHR$ (TY1-25
6*INT (TY1/256))
1260 DEF FN B$( )=CHR$ INT (TX2/2
56)+CHR$ (TX2-256*INT (TX2/256))
```

```
+CHR$ INT (TY2/256)+CHR$ (TY2-25
6*INT (TY2/256))
1270 LET A$=" ": RETURN
```

The functions and variables defined here will be discussed during the course of the commentary on the program.

MODULE 3.5.3

```
1280 REM ************************
1290 REM DRAW LINES
1300 REM ************************
1310 IF (X1<LEFT AND X2<LEFT) OR
 (X1>RIGHT AND Y2>RIGHT) OR (Y1>
TOP AND Y2>TOP) OR (Y1<BOTTOM AN
D Y2<BOTTOM) THEN LET OUT=1: RET
URN
1320 IF Y1>TOP THEN LET EDGE=TOP
1330 IF Y1<BOTTOM THEN LET EDGE=
BOTTOM
1340 IF Y1<BOTTOM OR Y1>TOP THEN
 LET X1=X1+(X2-X1)*(EDGE-Y1)/(Y2
-Y1): LET Y1=EDGE
1350 IF Y2>TOP THEN LET EDGE=TOP
1360 IF Y2<BOTTOM THEN LET EDGE=
BOTTOM
1370 IF Y2<BOTTOM OR Y2>TOP THEN
 LET X2=X2+(X1-X2)*(EDGE-Y2)/(Y1
-Y2): LET Y2=EDGE
1380 IF X1>RIGHT THEN LET EDGE=R
IGHT
1390 IF X1<LEFT THEN LET EDGE=LE
FT
1400 IF X1<LEFT OR X1>RIGHT THEN
 LET Y1=Y1+(Y2-Y1)*(EDGE-X1)/(X2
-X1): LET X1=EDGE
1410 IF X2>RIGHT THEN LET EDGE=R
IGHT
1420 IF X2<LEFT THEN LET EDGE=LE
FT
```

```
1430 IF X2<LEFT OR X2>RIGHT THEN
 LET Y2=Y2+(Y1-Y2)*(EDGE-X2)/(X1
-X2): LET X2=EDGE
1440 IF X1-LEFT>=0 AND X2-LEFT>=
0 AND X1-LEFT<=255 AND X2-LEFT<=
255 AND Y1-BOTTOM>=0 AND Y1-BOTT
OM<=167 AND Y2-BOTTOM>=0 AND Y2-
BOTTOM<=167 THEN PLOT X1-LEFT,Y1
-BOTTOM+8: DRAW INT (X2-X1),INT
(Y2-Y1)
1450 RETURN
```

The function of this module is to take two sets of co-ordinates, X1/Y1 and X2/Y2, and to decide whether any part of a line drawn between the two points so defined will pass across the screen. If any part of the line does fall on the screen, it is drawn, other parts of the line are rejected.

Commentary

Line 1310. The screen forms a window on the overall design being created and the borders of the area to which the screen points are stored in the variables TOP, BOTTOM, LEFT and RIGHT. If BOTTOM is set to 500 and LEFT to 500, the screen will set to display any pixels which fall between 500 and 755 horizontally and 500 and 667 vertically. The purpose of this program line is to disqualify from consideration any line in the design which both starts and finishes above, below or to one side of the area of the design covered by the screen.

Lines 1320-1330. If a line starts above or below the area covered by the screen, these two lines reset the variable EDGE to coincide with the top or bottom of the screen.

Line 1340. For lines which begin above or below the screen, this line calculates the horizontal position at which the line will pass the top or bottom edge. The formula in the first half of the line says nothing more complex than that if, for instance, the line in question passes through the top edge of the screen half way through its vertical component, it will also be halfway through its horizontal component. Clearly this will only hold true for straight lines.

Lines 1350-1430. The same procedure is carried out in relation to the co-ordinates Y1,X2 and Y2.

Line 1440. Since it is possible for a line not to lie entirely above, below or to one side of the screen and still not cross the screen itself, this program line checks that the co-ordinates calculated do in fact lie on the screen. If they do, then the first set of co-ordinates is plotted and a line is drawn to the second.

Testing Module 3.5.3

If this module is functioning correctly you should be able to RUN the program and initialise the variables. Having done this, stop the program and enter, in direct mode, 127/200 and 127/100 as values for X1/Y1 and X2/Y2. These four values should result, if you GOTO 1280, in the drawing of a line from the middle of the top edge of the screen to around the middle of the screen.

MODULE 3.5.4

```
1530 REM ************************
1540 REM CURSOR
1550 REM ************************
1560 LET ANGLE=0: LET S=1: GO SU
B 1820
1570 PRINT AT 21,18;"0QUIT1DEF2M
OVE";AT 21,0;"X1=";O1;AT 21,8;"Y
1=";O2: LET X=O1: LET Y=O2
1580 GO SUB 1660: IF T$="2" THEN
 GO SUB 1820: PRINT AT 21,18;"0Q
UIT1DEF2MOVE": LET X=O1: LET Y=O
2: GO TO 1570
1590 LET TTX1=X: LET TTY1=Y: IF
T$="0" THEN RETURN
1600 PRINT AT 21,0;"X2=";X;"   ";
AT 21,8;"Y2=";Y;"   ": PAUSE 50:
GO SUB 1660: IF T$="2" THEN GO S
UB 1820: PRINT AT 21,18;"0QUIT1D
EF2MOVE": LET X=O1: LET Y=O2: GO
 TO 1600
1610 IF T$="0" THEN RETURN
1620 LET X2=X: LET TX2=X: LET Y2
=Y: LET TY2=Y: LET X1=TTX1: LET
Y1=TTY1: LET TX1=X1: LET TY1=Y1:
 OVER 1: GO SUB 1280
1630 INPUT "OK? ";Q$: IF Q$="Y"
THEN OVER 0: LET A$=A$+FN A$()+F
N B$()
```

```
1640 GO SUB 1280: OVER 0: PRINT
AT 21,0;"X1";AT 21,8;"Y1": IF Q$
<>"Y" THEN PLOT OVER 1;TX1-LEFT,
TY1-BOTTOM+8: PLOT OVER 1;TX2-LE
FT,TY2-BOTTOM+8
1650 GO TO 1580
1660 PLOT BRIGHT 1; OVER 1;X-LEF
T,Y-BOTTOM+8: PAUSE 2: PLOT BRIG
HT 0; OVER 1;X-LEFT,Y-BOTTOM+8:
LET T$=INKEY$: IF T$="" THEN GO
TO 1660
1670 LET X=X+(T$="8")-(T$="5")
1680 LET X=X+10*(T$="I")-10*(T$=
"T")
1690 LET Y=Y+(T$="7")-(T$="6")
1700 LET Y=Y+10*(T$="U")-10*(T$=
"Y")
1710 IF X>RIGHT THEN LET X=RIGHT
1720 IF X<LEFT THEN LET X=LEFT
1730 IF Y>TOP THEN LET Y=TOP
1740 IF Y<BOTTOM THEN LET Y=BOTT
OM
1750 IF T$="1" THEN PLOT OVER 1;
X-LEFT,Y-BOTTOM+8: RETURN
1755 IF T$="0" OR T$="2" THEN RE
TURN
1760 PRINT AT 21,3;X;"   ";AT 21,
11;Y;"   "
1770 GO TO 1660
```

The purpose of this module is to allow the user to move a small cursor around the screen in order to set the start and finish co-ordinates of a line.

Commentary

Line 1560. Though the program is capable of shrinking the overall design by any specified factor and rotating it, lines can only be input with the design at normal size and unrotated. This line sets the angle of the design (ANGLE) and the reduction factor (S) accordingly, before calling up the module which draws the part of the design to which the user makes the screen point.

Line 1570. You may have noticed that the screen is only 168 pixels high, rather than the 176 permitted. This is to allow line 21 to be used to display the actual co-ordinates of the cursor in relation to the bottom left-hand corner of the overall design.

Line 1590. In the course of the program, five sets of variables are used at various points to store the same data, namely X/Y,X1/Y1,X2/Y2,TX1/TY1 and TTX1/TTY2. The simple reason for this is that at times the value of one co-ordinate is altered for some temporary purpose. The leading T is an indicator that this is intended as a temporary storage place. This line also permits the user to move the window pointed to by the screen after defining the beginning of a line. In this way lines may be defined which pass over more than one screen area.

Line 1630. Having drawn the specified line, the user is invited to confirm it or otherwise. If it is confirmed, the co-ordinates X1/Y1 and X2/Y2 are stored, in two byte form created by FN A$ and FN B$, in the undefined string A$.

Lines 1660-1770. You will recognise this as a fairly standard cursor moving routine. One difference is that apart from the cursor keys themselves, the keys immediately below them and to the right (TYUI) can be used to move the pixel cursor 10 places at a time, thus speeding up the process. Pressing 1 causes a return to an earlier part of the module, thus defining one of the sets of co-ordinates.

Testing Module 3.5.4
By entering a temporary line 1820 with Return and defining O1 and O2 in direct mode as 127 and 83 respectively, you should be able to call up this module and move the cursor around the screen, define two positions — you cannot yet move the screen in between the start and finish of the line — and see the line displayed for your confirmation or otherwise.

MODULE 3.5.5

```
1780 REM ************************
1790 REM ROTATE
1800 REM ************************
1810 INPUT "ANGLE?",ANGLE: LET A
NGLE=ANGLE*PI/180: INPUT "SCALE
FACTOR?",S: IF S=0 THEN LET S=1
```

```
1820 INPUT "CO-ORDINATES OF ORIG
IN?"'O1,O2: IF Z$="2" AND O1<127
 THEN LET O1=127
1830 IF Z$="2" AND O2<83 THEN LE
T O2=83
1840 LET LEFT=O1-127: LET BOTTOM
=O2-83: LET RIGHT=LEFT+255: LET
TOP=BOTTOM+167
1850 CLS
1860 FOR I=2 TO LEN A$ STEP 8
1870 IF I>LEN A$ THEN LET SEARCH
=0: GO TO 1970
1880 LET I1=I: LET X1=(FN A()-O1
)/S: LET I1=I1+2: LET Y1=(FN A()
-O2)/S: LET I1=I1+2: LET X2=(FN
A()-O1)/S: LET I1=I1+2: LET Y2=(
FN A()-O2)/S
1890 LET TX1=X1: LET TX2=X2: LET
 TY1=Y1: LET TY2=Y2
1900 LET X1=O1+INT (TX1*COS ANGL
E+TY1*SIN ANGLE)
1910 LET X2=O1+INT (TX2*COS ANGL
E+TY2*SIN ANGLE)
1920 LET Y1=O2+INT (-TX1*SIN ANG
LE+TY1*COS ANGLE)
1930 LET Y2=O2+INT (-TX2*SIN ANG
LE+TY2*COS ANGLE)
1940 IF SEARCH=1 THEN OVER 1
1950 GO SUB 1280: IF SEARCH=1 TH
EN GO SUB 1460: IF T$="0" THEN L
ET T$="": LET SEARCH=0: RETURN
1960 NEXT I: LET SEARCH=0
1970 INPUT "ENTER=CONTINUE/""CCC
=COPY";Q$
1980 IF Q$="CCC" THEN COPY
1990 RETURN
```

It is this module which allows the window represented by the screen to be moved around the design command.

Commentary
Line 1820. The position of the screen in relation to the design as a whole is defined by setting the position of the centre of the screen. Note also that when the program function is 2 only positions with positive co-ordinates are available to the user. That is, the user can only draw lines in parts of the design which have positive addresses. This is because negative addresses cannot be stored in A$ by the two functions FN A$ and FN B$. At other times during the program's execution, such as when a design is rotated, lines may be created whose ends have negative co-ordinates and these will be printed without problems if the screen window is set to point to them.

Line 1840. The borders of the screen are set to match the specified centre of the screen.

Lines 1860-1880. Using the function FN A, the values stored in A$ are translated back into numerical co-ordinates. They are translated into positions relative to the centre of the screen window. This distance is then multiplied by the scaling factor. The co-ordinates are then rotated around the centre of the screen through the required angle.

Lines 1890-1930. The procedure for moving a point with co-ordinates X and Y through an angle, say A, is to apply the formula: X2 = X*COS A + Y*SIN A and Y1 = −X*SIN A + Y*COS A.

Line 1940 The variable Search is used to indicate that the deletion module is to be called.

Testing Module 3.5.5
You should now be able to move the screen window over your design and also to move the screen in between the first and second set of co-ordinates when defining a line. You should also be able to print the overall design, or a part of it, at various scales and at various angles.

MODULE 3.5.6

```
1460 REM **********************
1470 REM DELETE LINES
1480 REM **********************
1490 PRINT OVER 0;AT 21,0;"YCONF
IRMNDELETE0QUIT": LET OUT=0: OVE
R 1: GO SUB 1280: GO SUB 1280: L
ET T$=INKEY$: IF OUT=1 THEN GO T
```

```
0 1510
1500 IF T$<>"0" AND T$<>"Y" AND
T$<>"N" THEN GO TO 1490
1510 OVER 0: IF T$="Y" OR OUT=1
THEN GO SUB 1280: RETURN
1520 OVER 1: GO SUB 1280: PAUSE
50: OVER 0: LET A$=A$( TO I-1)+A
$(I+8 TO ): LET I=I-8: RETURN
```

This module draws the line pointed to by the loop variable I in the previous module. The line is drawn twice with OVER set and the user is then given an opportunity to specify either that the line remains or that the program leaves the module or that the address of the relevant line is removed from A$. The line is flashed until one of these inputs is made.

Testing Module 3.5.6
You should now be able to delete lines.

Summary
This program is a useful tool in a variety of applications, given a little imagination. You can plan layouts, draw maps or simply mess about. In fact you can simulate many of the capabilities of more expensive graphics computers beloved of engineers and scientists in many fields. But do not forget that the program is also an example of an easily available technique applied to the Spectrum. The books are there for all of us, crammed with powerful ideas that help release the power of your micro.

Going Further
1) Could you combine this program with the techniques of shape drawing found in the Tangrams program, allowing the start address of certain common shapes to be specified in A$?

2) The program would be more flexible if it made provision to print out text as part of the overall design. Once again the co-ordinates would need to be stored in A$.

CHAPTER 4

EASING EDUCATION – The Spectrum as a home tutor

In this chapter we shall consider three programs which enable the Spectrum to be applied in the field of home education. The first of these, MultiQ, is a program designed to allow the user to input a series of questions and answers which are then used as the basis of randomly generated multiple choice tests. The second program is Words, a basic reading tutor. Lastly, Where?, teaches you the location of cities in any country you care to program in.

The object of these programs is to give an idea of what can be accomplished without too much effort in the area of home education. Even so, unless you intend to buy a range of software on cassette, with specialist programs dedicated to individual subjects coming complete with their own files of data, the usefulness of your education programs will always depend on the amount of work you are prepared to put into them. The best multiple choice question program in the world is not much use unless at some stage you are prepared to sit down and feed in enough questions to make it interesting.

If you are prepared to do a little work in giving such programs the data to work with they can often be spectacularly successful for the simple reason that they work at the pace of the person who is attempting to learn, show no signs of impatience when the progress is slow and are always ready for just one more try.

4.1 MultiQ

This program is a favourite of mine. When I wrote it I was satisfied that it was a competent piece of work that would do the job that it was designed for. It was not until I first entered a mass a questions and answers and tried it out on people that I realised that such programs make learning as addictive as any game.

Like Unifile, this program is a chameleon, designed to change its colour to suit your need. At one moment you may wish it to be a French tutor, offering a variety of French words as possible translations of a single English word. Later on you may have it asking fairly complex questions on 19th century history, giving a series of dates as possible answers. The aim of the program is to enable you to do all these and more without making changes to the program itself.

The program is also interesting for the manner in which it stores its data. Unifile, you will remember, kept its data in a single long file, keeping track of each entry by means of a pointer array. MultiQ stores its data on a series of two dimensional arrays. i.e. A$(1000,10) would provide 1,000 spaces 10 characters long. This has disadvantages in that it becomes impossible to use the space to the maximum, as noted before. In this case, however, the user does have some choice as to the form of the items to be stored and, if an item looks as if it is going to be much longer than all the rest it can usually be shortened rather than enlarging the planned array to fit it. If the space-saving argument is not crucial, two dimensional arrays have the advantage that each item has a clearly identifiable place in the file, which makes finding the data easier.

There remains the problem, however, that such an array can be clumsy when it comes to deleting items or inserting them in the middle, since all the succeeding items must be moved one place to cover the resulting gap or make room for the new entry. Since there is no command which moves the whole block within an array, this has to be done item by item, a time-consuming process.

We can overcome the problem in relation to inserting items by simply not putting new items into the middle of the array in their correct place but inserting them into the first available space and leaving it to a pointer array to tell us the order in which the items should be taken.

Deletion is not so simple. The program is not going to be much use if items cannot be taken out if they are wrong and, whichever way you look at it, if the first item in the array is removed that leaves an empty line. Very soon, if you need to delete items with any regularity, you will end up with an array that is riddled with empty spaces and no room at the end to place any new items of data.

The solution adopted here is to keep a record of the position of any items deleted from the file and to use that record as an indicator of where any new entries may be placed. In other words, if the last item to be deleted was in position one, the next item to be input will be placed in position one. If, as will often be the case, there are no holes left in the array, the program will place the new item at the end of the current items. Simple when you get the idea and, as you will see when you come to enter the program, not difficult in practice.

MODULE 4.1.1

```
1000 REM ************************
1010 REM MENU
1020 REM ************************
1030 BORDER 1: INK 0: PAPER 7: C
LS : PRINT "            MultiQ"
1040 PRINT '"COMMANDS AVAILABLE:
"
1050 PRINT '"1)INITIALISE"
1060 PRINT '"2)INPUT NEW ITEMS"
1070 PRINT '"3)SEARCH/DELETE"
1080 PRINT '"4)ENTER NEW TYPES"
1090 PRINT '"5)GENERATE QUESTION
S"
1100 PRINT '"6)DISPLAY OR RESET
SCORE"
1110 PRINT '"7)STOP"
1120 INPUT "Which do you require
?";Z$
1140 CLS
1150 IF Z$="1" THEN GO SUB 1270
1160 IF Z$="2" THEN GO SUB 1800
1170 IF Z$="3" THEN GO SUB 2460
1180 IF Z$="4" THEN GO SUB 1670
1190 IF Z$="5" THEN GO SUB 2880
1200 IF Z$="6" THEN GO SUB 3380
1210 IF Z$="7" THEN GO TO 1240
1220 CLS
1230 GO TO 1000
1240 PRINT AT 7,12;"MultiQ"
1250 INPUT "Have you entered any
 new           information which yo
u wish to   save? (Y/N)";Q$
1260 IF Q$="Y" THEN SAVE "MULTIQ
": BEEP 1,40: PRINT AT 12,0;"REW
IND, THEN ""ENTER"" TO VERIFY.":
 PAUSE 0: VERIFY "MULTIQ": PRINT
 '"VERIFIED"
1265 STOP
```

This is a standard menu module.

MODULE 4.1.2

```
1270 REM ************************
1280 REM INITIALISE
1290 REM ************************
1295 DIM O$(32)
1300 DIM C$(2,20)
1310 LET I$=CHR$ 0+CHR$ 1+CHR$ 0
+CHR$ 2
1320 DIM C(2)
1330 LET L$="
          "
1340 LET ITEMS=2
1350 LET P$="     "
1360 LET ENDITEM=3
1370 LET RIGHT=0
1380 LET QTOT=0
1390 INK 1: PRINT "          TEA
CHER"
1400 PRINT '"NAME FOR ANSWER:";
1410 INPUT C$(1)
1420 PRINT C$(1)
1430 PRINT '"LENGTH OF LONGEST A
NSWER:";
1440 INPUT C(1)
1450 LET C(1)=C(1)+1
1460 PRINT C(1)-1
1470 PRINT ''"NAME FOR QUESTION:
";
1480 INPUT C$(2)
1490 PRINT C$(2)
1500 PRINT '"LENGTH OF LONGEST Q
UESTION:";
1510 INPUT C(2)
1520 PRINT C(2)
1530 INPUT "Are these correct? (
Y/N)";Q$
```

```
1550 CLS
1560 IF Q$<>"Y" THEN GO TO 1270
1570 DIM F$(C(1))
1580 DIM G$(C(2))
1590 LET C1=C(1)+C(2)
1600 LET C2=INT (25000/C1)
1610 DIM A$(C2,C(1))
1620 DIM B$(C2,C(2))
1625 LET A$(1,1)=CHR$ 0
1630 LET A$(2,1)=CHR$ 255
1640 LET TYPES=0
1650 DIM D$(10,20)
1660 DIM D(2,10)
1670 PRINT "INPUT ";"EXTRA " AND
 (TYPES>0);"TYPES OF ANSWER:"
1680 PRINT '"(""ZZZ"" TO QUIT)"
1720 INPUT Q$
1730 IF Q$="ZZZ" THEN RETURN
1740 LET D$(TYPES+1)=Q$
1750 PRINT TYPES+1;") ";D$(TYPES
+1)
1755 LET TYPES=TYPES+1
1760 IF TYPES<10 THEN GO TO 1720
1770 PRINT '"ONLY 10 TYPES ALLOW
ED."
1780 PRINT '"Press any key to co
ntinue."
1785 PAUSE 0
1790 RETURN
```

This module sets up variables and re-dimensions the arrays to suit new applications of the program.

Commentary

Lines 1390-1580. Data is stored in the program under the headings of questions, answers and types, with the names given to each defined by the user. If the tests are to take the form of an English word accompanied by five possible French translations, you might input 'French' in response to 'name for answer' and

'English' is response to 'name for question'. You must also decide upon the maximum length for questions and answers for the particular application.

Lines 1590-1620. The two main arrays in which the data will be stored (A$ = answers, B$ = questions) are re-dimensioned to take up the whole of the available memory space regardless of the length of the lines in each. The shorter the items the more lines there will be.

Lines 1650-1790. Each item can be given a type e.g noun, verb etc. in the case of a French test. These types can be used to make testing more stringent later on. Up to 10 types can be specified and their names will be stored in D$. The array D will be used to record how many items of each type there are and where they are grouped in the file. Note that you can omit provision for types by entering ZZZ before any type names are entered. In this case the program makes no further reference to types.

Testing Module 4.1.2
When run, this module should request headings and types.

MODULE 4.1.3

```
1800 REM ************************
1810 REM INPUT OF NEW ITEMS
1820 REM ************************
1830 PRINT "              NEW ITEMS"
1840 PRINT PAPER 6;'C$(1)
1850 INPUT F$
1860 IF ITEMS<>C2 THEN GO TO 189
0
1870 PRINT '"NO ROOM FOR MORE IT
EMS."
1880 GO TO 2130
1890 IF F$(1 TO 3)="ZZZ" THEN GO
 TO 2130
1900 PRINT INVERSE 1;F$
1910 PRINT PAPER 6;'C$(2)
1920 INPUT G$
1930 PRINT INVERSE 1;G$
1940 IF D$(1,1)<>" " THEN GO TO
1970
1950 LET T=0
1960 GO TO 2040
1970 PRINT '"TYPES:"
```

```
1980 FOR I=1 TO TYPES
1990 PRINT I;") ";D$(I)
2000 NEXT I
2010 INPUT T
2030 PRINT '"TYPE SELECTED:";D$(
T)
2040 INPUT "Are these correct? (
Y/N)";Q$
2060 CLS
2070 IF Q$<>"Y" THEN GO TO 1830
2075 IF T<>0 THEN LET D(1,T)=D(1
,T)+1
2080 LET F$=CHR$ T+F$
2090 GO SUB 2190
2100 GO SUB 2330
2110 LET ITEMS=ITEMS+1
2120 GO TO 1800
2130 LET TOTAL=2
2140 FOR I=1 TO 10
2150 LET D(2,I)=TOTAL
2160 LET TOTAL=TOTAL+D(1,I)
2170 NEXT I
2180 RETURN
```

This module accepts new inputs under the headings and types specified in the previous module.

Commentary
Line 1860. C2 is the number of lines in the main array.

Line 1940. The user is only asked to specify a type if there is at least one main type name stored in D$.

Line 2080. The type — 0 if no types are specified — is added to the beginning of the answer in the form of a single character indicator.

Line 2130-2170. This loop transfers a cumulative total of the sums in the first column in the array D, i.e. the numbers of items of each type, to the second column in the same array. Since items are stored in type order this effectively stores the start address of each type group in the second column.

Testing Module 4.1.3
The program should accept the input of an item, though it cannot be placed into the array.

MODULE 4.1.4

```
2190 REM ***********************
2200 REM BINARY SEARCH
2210 REM ***********************
2215 DEF FN A()=256*CODE I$(2*S-
1)+CODE I$(2*S)
2220 LET POWER=INT (LN ITEMS/LN
2)
2230 LET S=2^POWER
2240 FOR I=POWER-1 TO 0 STEP -1
2250 LET P=FN A()
2260 LET S=S+(2^I)*(A$(P)<F$)-(2
^I)*(A$(P)>F$)
2270 IF S<2 THEN LET S=2
2280 IF S>ITEMS-1 THEN LET S=ITE
MS-1
2290 NEXT I
2300 LET P=FN A()
2310 IF A$(P)>F$ THEN LET S=S-1
2320 RETURN
```

This module determines the correct position of new items in the existing order and is parallel to the search module in Unifile. The method used is again a binary search.

MODULE 4.1.5

```
2330 REM ***********************
2340 REM INSERTION
2350 REM ***********************
2360 IF LEN P$=4 THEN GO TO 2400
2370 LET PLACE=256*CODE P$(3)+CO
DE P$(4)
```

```
2380 LET P$=P$( TO 2)+P$(5 TO )
2390 GO TO 2420
2400 LET PLACE=ENDITEM
2410 LET ENDITEM=ENDITEM+1
2420 LET A$(PLACE)=F$
2430 LET B$(PLACE)=G$
2440 LET I$=I$( TO 2*S)+CHR$ INT
 (PLACE/256)+CHR$ INT (PLACE-256
*INT (PLACE/256))+I$(2*S+1 TO )
2450 RETURN
```

The new item is inserted into the first available space and its address is stored in the array I$.

Commentary

Lines 2360-2390. P$ stores the addresses of holes in the array. When there are no such holes the length of the string is 4 — the minimum in order to avoid line 2380 coming up with an error message. Provided that P$ is longer than four characters, the second pair is translated into an address.

Lines 2400-2410. If there are no gaps indicated by P$ the new item is placed at the end of the file in the first empty space.

Lines 2420-2440. The answer and the question, F$ and G$, are placed into line PLACE of arrays A$ and B$ respectively. Note that PLACE registers the actual address of the item in the file, not its correct position in the order, which is held by the variable S. This is determined by the binary search. Since the type has been appended to the beginning of the answer, the order is first of all based upon type.

Testing Module 4.1.5

Enter a series of items of the same type: they should be entered in reverse alphabetical order i.e. e,d,c,b,a. The items should be placed in the arrays in the order in which you input them. Now examine I$. You should be able to translate character pairs into pointers to positions 5,4,3,2,1 or however many items you input in reverse alphabetical order. Remember that items are sorted on the basis of the answers.

MODULE 4.1.6

```
2460 REM ************************
2470 REM USER SEARCH
2480 REM ************************
2485 IF ITEMS=2 THEN RETURN
2490 PRINT "                SEARCH"
2495 PRINT AT 21,15;"TOTAL ITEMS
:";ITEMS-2
2500 PRINT AT 3,0;"COMMANDS AVAI
LABLE:"
2510 PRINT '">""ENTER"" FOR NEXT
 ITEM"
2520 PRINT ">POSITIVE OR NEGATIV
E NUMBER TO MOVE POINTER"
2530 PRINT ">""DDD"" TO DELETE I
TEM"
2540 PRINT ">""ZZZ"" TO QUIT FUN
CTION"
2550 PRINT 'L$
2580 LET S=2
2600 LET P=FN A( )
2610 PRINT AT 12,0;"ENTRY No. ";
S-1
2620 PRINT 'A$(P,2 TO )
2630 PRINT B$(P)
2640 IF CODE(A$(P,1))=0 THEN GO
TO 2660
2650 PRINT 'D$(CODE A$(P,1))
2660 INPUT S$
2670 IF S$="DDD" THEN GO SUB 278
0: RETURN
2690 IF S$="ZZZ" THEN RETURN
2700 IF S$<>"" THEN GO TO 2740
2710 LET S=S+1
2720 IF S=ITEMS THEN RETURN
2730 GO TO 2600
2740 LET S=S+VAL S$
2750 IF S>=ITEMS THEN RETURN
```

```
2760 IF S<2 THEN LET S=2
2770 GO TO 2600
```

The purpose of this module is to allow the user to page through the entries and delete unwanted ones. The module is simpler than the search module in the Unifile program, having the capability to display the next entry or move on a specified number of items. It does not actually search.

MODULE 4.1.7

```
2780 REM *************************
2790 REM DELETIONS
2800 REM *************************
2810 LET P=FN A( )
2815 LET D(1,CODE A$(P,1))=D(1,C
ODE A$(P,1))-1
2820 LET A$(P)=""
2830 LET B$(P)=""
2840 LET I$=I$( TO 2*S-2)+I$(2*S
+1 TO )
2850 LET ITEMS=ITEMS-1
2860 LET P$=P$( TO 2)+CHR$ INT (
P/256)+CHR$ INT (P-256*INT (P/25
6))+P$(3 TO )
2865 GO SUB 2130
2870 RETURN
```

This module removes items from the file and stores the address of the resultant gap in P$.

Commentary
Lines 2810-2860. Since the variable S is pointing to the item on display, it is used to extract an address from the pointer array, I$, and the lines at this address in A$ and B$ are emptied. The address is removed from I$ and placed into P$.

Line 2865. The start addresses of the various groups of types are re-adjusted.

Testing Module 4.1.7
Delete an item and check that the rest of the data is still in a sensible order.

MODULE 4.1.8

```
2880 REM ***********************
2890 REM RANDOM QUESTIONS
2900 REM ***********************
2910 LET QUESTION=0
2920 PRINT "             QUESTIONS"
2930 PRINT '"DO YOU WISH POSSIBL
E ANSWERS TO BE DRAWN ONLY FROM 
THE SAME      ANSWER TYPE? (Y/N)"
2940 INPUT Q$: CLS
2960 IF Q$="Y" THEN LET QUESTION
=1
2970 DIM Q(5)
2980 LET Q1=INT (RND*(ITEMS-2)+2
)
2990 LET S=Q1
3000 LET P=FN A()
3010 LET Q2=INT (RND*5+1)
3020 LET Q(Q2)=P
3030 LET START=2
3040 LET NUMBER=ITEMS-2
3045 IF CODE(A$(P,1))=0 THEN GO 
TO 3080
3050 IF QUESTION=0 OR D(1,CODE A
$(P,1))<5 THEN  GO TO 3080
3060 LET START=D(2,CODE A$(P,1))
3070 LET NUMBER=D(1,CODE A$(P,1)
)
3080 FOR I=1 TO 5
3090 IF I=Q2 THEN GO TO 3170
3100 LET S=INT (RND*NUMBER+START
)
3110 LET P=FN A()
3120 IF P=Q(Q2) THEN GO TO 3100
3130 FOR J=1 TO I
3140 IF P=Q(J) THEN GO TO 3100
3150 NEXT J
3160 LET Q(I)=P
3170 NEXT I
3180 PRINT AT 1,0;C$(2)
3190 PRINT 'B$(Q(Q2))
3200 PRINT 'L$''
```

```
3205 PRINT C$(1)''
3210 FOR I=1 TO 5
3220 PRINT I;"> ";A$(Q(I),2 TO )
3230 NEXT I
3240 PRINT ''"WHICH DO YOU THINK
 IS THE RIGHT ANSWER?"'"TYPE IN
THE NUMBER:";
3250 LET QTOT=QTOT+1
3260 INPUT ANSWER: PRINT "";ANSW
ER
3270 IF ANSWER=Q2 THEN GO TO 330
0
3280 PRINT '"INCORRECT. THE RIGH
T ANSWER WAS:";A$(Q(Q2),2 TO )
3290 GO TO 3320
3300 FOR I=14 TO 20
3302 PRINT AT I,0;O$
3304 NEXT I
3306 FLASH 1: PRINT AT 8+ANSWER,
3;A$(Q(ANSWER),2 TO ): PRINT AT
16,10;"CORRECT": PAUSE 50: FLASH
 0
3310 LET RIGHT=RIGHT+1
3320 PRINT """ENTER"" for new qu
estion or      ""ZZZ"" to quit fu
nction."
3340 INPUT Q$
3350 CLS
3360 IF Q$="ZZZ" THEN RETURN
3370 GO TO 2970
```

This module sets up the multiple answer tests on the basis of the items stored.

Commentary

Lines 2880-3000. The user is given the option as to whether the five answers to each question are drawn from the whole file or only from items of the same type.

Lines 2980-3000. A random item is chosen from the file.

Lines 3010-3020. The addresses of the five answers will be stored in the array Q. The address of the correct answer is placed into a random position in that array.

Lines 3030-3170. When creating a random number within certain limits it is necessary to know two things: firstly the base on which the number is to be built and secondly the range above that base within which the random number should fall. The RND function of the Spectrum produces a pseudo-random value between 0 and 1, so that a number having the form X + INT(Y*RND) will be capable of varying between X and X + Y-1. The minimum value that Y*RND can take may be less than one so that INT(Y*RND) will equal zero. The maximum value of INT(Y*RND) is Y – 1 since RND can never quite equal 1.

In this section of the program a number of random addresses must be generated and this will be done on the basis of the variables START and NUMBER. If the user has specified that answers be drawn from the whole file rather than from a specific type, START is set to 2 — the first usable item after the beginning of file marker. NUMBER is set to the real number of items — ITEMS minus the two file markers.

If the user has specified only answers of the same type, START is set to the first address in that group in which the random choice fell and number is set to the number of items within that group. This is only done if there are five or more items in the group in question. The answer landed upon is compared with the original answer to see that it is not the same and then with the rest of the answers chosen randomly. If the new random choice is not a duplication its address is placed into Q in a random position.

Lines 3180-3230. The question is printed at the top of the screen; the answers are printed at the bottom.

Testing Module 4.1.8
Enter some questions and answers and test yourself.

MODULE 4.1.9

```
3380 REM ***********************
3390 REM SCORE
3400 REM ***********************
3410 PRINT "             SCORE"
3420 IF QTOT<>0 THEN GO TO 3470
3430 PRINT ''''"      NO SCORE Y
ET."
3440 PRINT '"    Any key to conti
nue."
```

```
3450 PAUSE 0
3460 RETURN
3470 PRINT '"TOTAL QUESTIONS:";Q
TOT
3480 PRINT '"CORRECT:";RIGHT
3490 PRINT "ASSESSMENT:";INT (((
RIGHT-QTOT/5)/(QTOT*.8))*100);"
PER CENT."
3500 PRINT '"DO YOU WISH TO ZERO
 SCORE? (Y/N)"
3510 INPUT Q$
3520 IF Q$<>"Y" THEN RETURN
3530 LET QTOT=0
3540 LET RIGHT=0
3550 RETURN
```

This module is designed to display the score so far and reset it on request.

Commentary

Line 3490. This line is an attempt to give a sensible assessment of the score given the fact that random button pushing should result in a score of 20% on average. This hypothetical 20% is subtracted from both the total questions and the right answers and the assessment is made on the rest.

Testing Module 4.1.9

If you have previously tested Module 8 the variables have already been set. Calling up this module will give you a score and an assessment.

Summary

This is actually quite a powerful program but you will only confirm that fact for yourself if you give it some material. Quite apart from its uses as an educational tool it is also a simple demonstration of a method of speeding up access to arrays by removing the neccessity to telescope the file every time a deletion is made. The core of the program could very easily be applied to a wide variety of uses where the speed of access to items is more important than saving every last byte of memory space.

Going Further

1) The program as it stands does not give much of a reward for right answers or good scores. Could you program in some kind of visual reward at an appropriate point?

2) Programming is a fairly solitary practice but using a program like this one can be improved by some co-operation with others. Persuade someone else to buy this book and set them to building up a file on physics while you tackle history.

3) Could you add a more powerful search function based on the search function in the Unifile program?

4.2 Words

The moral of this program is that when you have a method which works well, adapt it to perform a variety of tasks, even if it looks suspiciously like other programs you have written before. This program is a take-off of MultiQ, the only real difference being that its questions take the form of pictures. It was meant to be a reading tutor but of course it is equally applicable to any other topic where everything needs to be presented visually and questions have to be asked.

The capacity of the program is fairly limited since the small picture has a space set aside for it of 400 characters. The pictures themselves are those generated by the Artist program. This means that the 400 character string represents a packed version of something which originally had a maximum of around 120 characters. The design must use only the lower half of the screen.

MODULE 4.2.1

```
1000 REM ***********************
1010 REM MENU
1020 REM ***********************
1030 BORDER 1: INK 0: PAPER 6: C
LS
1040 PRINT "               WORDS"
1050 PRINT '"COMMANDS AVAILABLE:
"
1060 PRINT '"1)INITIALISE"
1070 PRINT '"2)INPUT NEW ITEMS"
1080 PRINT '"3)SEARCH/DELETE"
1090 PRINT '"5)GENERATE QUESTION
S"
1100 PRINT '"6)DISPLAY OR RESET 
SCORE"
1110 PRINT '"7)STOP"
```

```
1120 INPUT "Which do you require
?";Z$
1130 CLS
1140 IF Z$="1" THEN GO SUB 1260
1150 IF Z$="2" THEN GO SUB 1390
1160 IF Z$="3" THEN GO SUB 1680
1170 IF Z$="5" THEN GO SUB 2010
1180 IF Z$="6" THEN GO SUB 2340
1190 IF Z$="7" THEN GO TO 1220
1200 CLS
1210 GO TO 1000
1220 PRINT AT 7,12;"WORDS"
1230 INPUT "Have you entered any
 new          information which yo
u wish to    save? (Y/N)";Q$
1240 IF Q$="Y" THEN SAVE "WORDS"
: PRINT AT 10,0;"REWIND, THEN AN
Y KEY TO VERIFY.": PAUSE 0: VERI
FY "WORDS"
1250 STOP
```

This is a standard menu module.

MODULE 4.2.2

```
1260 REM ************************
1270 REM INITIALISE
1280 REM ************************
1290 DIM Q$(32)
1300 LET L$="____________________
____________________"
1310 LET ITEMS=0
1320 LET I$="      "
1330 LET ENDITEM=1
1340 LET RIGHT=0
1350 LET QTOT=0
1360 DIM A$(50,15): DIM B$(50,40
0): DIM C$(15)
```

```
1370 DIM B(100)
1380 RETURN
```

This contains the program variables. The arrays are used to contain the packed string and the associated word.

MODULE 4.2.3

```
2620 REM ************************
2630 REM PRINT PACKED STRING
2640 REM ************************
2650 BORDER 1: PAPER 7: CLS : PR
INT AT 1,1;: LET SCREEN=0: LET C
OUNTER=1
2660 IF P$(COUNTER)=CHR$ 255 THE
N LET COUNTER=COUNTER+1: IF P$(C
OUNTER)<>CHR$ 0 THEN PRINT O$( T
O CODE P$(COUNTER));: LET SCREEN
=SCREEN+CODE P$(COUNTER): PRINT
"  " AND SCREEN/30=INT (SCREEN/3
0);: LET COUNTER=COUNTER+1: IF C
OUNTER<=LEN P$ THEN GO TO 2660
2670 IF COUNTER>LEN P$ THEN GO T
O 2710
2680 IF P$(COUNTER)=CHR$ 0 THEN
LET COUNTER=COUNTER+1
2690>LET SCREEN=SCREEN+1: INVERS
E CODE P$(COUNTER+2): PRINT P$(C
OUNTER);: POKE (23296-32*(PEEK 2
3689)-PEEK 23688+32),CODE P$(COU
NTER+1): INVERSE 0: IF SCREEN/30
=INT (SCREEN/30) THEN PRINT "  "
;
2700 LET COUNTER=COUNTER+3: IF C
OUNTER<=LEN P$ THEN GO TO 2660
2710 PAPER 7: INK 1: RETURN
```

This module is lifted straight out of the Artist program and reprints a packed string.

MODULE 4.2.4

```
1560 REM ************************
1570 REM INSERTION
1580 REM ************************
1590 IF LEN I$=4 THEN GO TO 1630
1600 LET PLACE=256*CODE I$(3)+CO
DE I$(4)
1610 LET I$=I$( TO 2)+I$(5 TO )
1620 GO TO 1650
1630 LET PLACE=ENDITEM
1640 LET ENDITEM=ENDITEM+1
1650 LET A$(PLACE)=N$
1660 LET B$(PLACE)=P$: LET B(PLA
CE)=LEN P$
1670 RETURN
```

This has the same structure as the insertion module in the previous program except that the string recording holes in the array is called I$ and the address of the new entry is not stored in a pointer array. With only 50 entries it seemed unnecessary to have a complex search function to establish a correct order of entries.

MODULE 4.2.5

```
1390 REM ************************
1400 REM INPUT OF NEW ITEMS
1410 REM ************************
1420 PRINT "              NEW ITEMS"
1430 INPUT "Name of Picture to b
e loaded     from tape? (ZZZ TO Q
UIT)";N$
1440 PRINT ''"PRESS ANY KEY THEN
 START TAPE.": PAUSE 0: PRINT ''
"           LOADING NOW": LOAD N$
 DATA P$()
```

```
1450 GO SUB 2620
1460 INPUT "Do you want this pic
ture?(Y/N)";Q$
1470 IF Q$<>"Y" THEN RETURN
1480 INPUT "Word to go with this
 picture?";W$
1490 PRINT AT 21,0;W$
1500 INPUT "Is this correct? (Y/
N)";Q$
1510 CLS : IF Q$="N" THEN GO TO
1480
1520 GO SUB 1560: LET ITEMS=ITEM
S+1
1530 INPUT "Do you want to input
 another     picture? (Y/N)";Q$
1540 IF Q$="N" THEN RETURN
1550 GO TO 1420
```

This module picks up from tape the packed string which contains the design, prints it, accepts the word which corresponds to it and finally stores it.

Testing Module 4.2.5

Having entered several familiar looking modules without testing their function you are now in a position to check that the program will pick up arrays from tape which have been created and saved using the Artist program, display the design they contain and store it in the memory.

MODULE 4.2.6

```
1680 REM ***********************
1690 REM USER SEARCH
1700 REM ***********************
1710 IF ITEMS=0 THEN RETURN
1720 LET S=1
1730 IF B$(S,1)=" " AND S<50 THE
N LET S=S+1: GO TO 1730
1740 IF S=50 AND B$(S,1)=" " THE
N RETURN
1750 CLS : DIM P$(B(S)): LET P$=
B$(S,1 TO B(S)): GO SUB 2620: PR
INT AT 21,0;A$(S)
```

```
1760 PRINT AT 0,0;"            S
EARCH"
1770 PRINT '"COMMANDS AVAILABLE:
"
1780 PRINT '">""ENTER"" FOR NEXT
 ITEM"
1790 PRINT ">POSITIVE OR NEGATIV
E NUMBER TO MOVE POINTER"
1800 PRINT ">""DDD"" TO DELETE I
TEM"
1810 PRINT ">""ZZZ"" TO QUIT FUN
CTION"
1820 PRINT 'L$
1830 INPUT S$
1840 IF S$="DDD" THEN GO SUB 193
0: RETURN
1850 IF S$="ZZZ" THEN RETURN
1860 IF S$<>"" THEN GO TO 1890
1870 LET S=S+1
1880 GO TO 1730
1890 LET S=S+VAL S$
1900 IF S>=50 THEN RETURN
1910 IF S<1 THEN LET S=1
1920 GO TO 1730
```

Again this is a simplified version of the search module taken from the previous program. When displaying a particular entry it does not first seek the address from a pointer array but simply begins at line one of the main array and prints whatever is there, unless the first character position is a space, in which case the line is empty and the module moves on to the next line.

Testing Module 4.2.6
You should be able to page through the entries stored, forwards or backwards.

MODULE 4.2.7

```
1930 REM ************************
1940 REM DELETIONS
1950 REM ************************
```

```
1960 LET A$(S)=""
1970 LET B$(S)=""
1980 LET ITEMS=ITEMS-1
1990 LET I$=I$( TO 2)+CHR$ INT (
S/256)+CHR$ INT (S-256*INT (S/25
6))+I$(3 TO )
2000 RETURN
```

This module allows the user to delete entries and is a simplified version of the same module in the previous program.

Testing Module 4.2.7
You should now be able to delete entries at will.

MODULE 4.2.8

```
2010 REM *************************
2020 REM RANDOM QUESTIONS
2030 REM *************************
2040 LET QUESTION=0
2050 DIM Q(5)
2060 LET Q1=INT (RND*ITEMS+1)
2070 LET Q2=INT (RND*5+1)
2080 LET Q(Q2)=Q1
2090 FOR I=1 TO 5
2100 IF I=Q2 THEN GO TO 2170
2110 LET S=INT (RND*ITEMS+1)
2120 IF S=Q(Q2) THEN GO TO 2110
2130 FOR J=1 TO I
2140 IF S=Q(J) THEN GO TO 2110
2150 NEXT J
2160 LET Q(I)=S
2170 NEXT I
2180 DIM P$(B(Q1)): LET P$=B$(Q1
): GO SUB 2620
2190 PRINT AT 0,0;
```

```
2200 FOR I=1 TO 5: DIM T$(32): L
ET T$=A$(Q(I))
2210 PRINT INK 9; PAPER 7-I;T$
2220 NEXT I
2230 PRINT '"WHICH ONE?"
2240 LET QTOT=QTOT+1
2250 INPUT C$: PRINT C$: IF C$=A
$(Q1) THEN GO TO 2270
2260 PRINT '"WRONG:";A$(Q1): GO
TO 2300
2270 FOR I=0 TO 10: LET I1=I-8*(
I>7): PRINT AT I,0; OVER 1; PAPE
R I1;O$: NEXT I
2280 FLASH 1: PRINT AT Q2-1,13;A
$(Q1): PRINT AT 10,10;"RIGHT!":
PAUSE 200: FLASH 0
2290 LET RIGHT=RIGHT+1
2300 INPUT """ENTER"" for new qu
estion or      ""ZZZ"" to stop";Q
$
2310 CLS
2320 IF Q$="ZZZ" OR q$="zzz" TH
EN GO TO 2520
2330 GO TO 2050
```

This module generates the random questions and possible answers. It is less complex than the equivalent module in the previous program because there is no provision for types of entries.

Commentary

Line 2200-2280. Note how it is possible to make the presentation of the questions and the reward for a right answer visually attractive without any great effort. In these lines loop variables are used to set background colours to add interest to the screen.

Testing Module 4.2.8

The program should now be capable of generating questions.

MODULE 4.2.9

```
2340 REM ***********************
2350 REM SCORE
2360 REM ***********************
2370 PRINT "            SCORE"
2380 IF QTOT<>0 THEN GO TO 2430
2390 PRINT ''''"      NO SCORE Y
ET."
2400 PRINT '"   Any key to conti
nue."
2410 PAUSE 0
2420 RETURN
2430 PRINT '"TOTAL QUESTIONS:";Q
TOT
2440 PRINT '"CORRECT:";RIGHT
2450 DEF FN A()=INT (((RIGHT-QTO
T/5)/(QTOT*.8))*100): PRINT '"AS
SESSMENT:";FN A();" PER CENT."
2460 PRINT '"DO YOU WISH TO ZERO
 SCORE? (Y/N)"
2470 INPUT Q$
2480 IF Q$<>"Y" THEN RETURN
2490 LET QTOT=0
2500 LET RIGHT=0
2510 RETURN
```

This is the score module taken from the previous program with one small change.

Commentary
Line 2450. The assessment, rather than being printed out directly, is stored in the variable ASS for later use.

Testing Module 4.2.9
You should now be able to call up a score from the menu.

MODULE 4.2.10

```
2520 REM ***********************
```

```
2530 REM BYE
2540 REM ************************
2550 CLS : LET I1=0: LET I2=1: P
APER 9
2560 FOR I=1 TO 100
2570 LET I1=I1+1-25*(I1=24)
2580 LET I2=I2+1-8*(I2=7)
2590 POKE 23692,255: INK I2: PRI
NT 'TAB I1;"GOODBYE!";
2600 NEXT I: PRINT " YOU SCORED
";FN A()
2610 INK 0: PAPER 7: STOP
```

This module prints out a slightly less boring farewell to the program and calls upon the function defined in the scoring module to give a final assessment.

Commentary
Line 2590. Note the use of this poke, which is used to prevent the scroll function stopping after 22 lines have been printed. Memory address 23692 is used by the Spectrum to record the number of lines which remain to be printed before the user is asked if scrolling should continue.

Testing Module 4.2.10
This module can only be called up from the module which generates questions.

Summary
This again is a program which requires some work if it is to be of any use since the small designs it uses do take some time to create. In creating the designs it is especially important to prepare properly before recording them with the Artist program. Use of squared paper will enable you to count the number of characters in the design. Anything over 100 or with the characters too scattered over the screen is unlikely to fit into the 400 character space set aside for the packed string. You will probably have noted that the part of the program which administers the test is rather cut off from the other functions. This is so that the adult can start the test off and leave it knowing that the child is unlikely to re-enter the main program and create havoc, or cheat. Before the test is started it is probably best if the CAPS LOCK is set to lower case, since children will tend to be more familiar with letters in that form. In order for this to work the words associated with each picture must also have been entered in lower case.

If you do not have any children of the right age you could always design yourself a set of characters representing electrical components and set the program to work teaching you to identify simple electronic circuits. As I said before, if you have something that works, adapt it.

Going Further

1) If you do not really need a record of the inverse characteristic for each character in the packed string you could either increase the number of designs the program can store or increase their complexity.

2) This is another case where co-operation with other Spectrum owners in the swapping of designs could save you a lot of effort.

4.3 Where?

This is an uncomplicated program which quite effectively tests your knowledge of geography, or at least of the location of cities in a range of countries. To use the program you will have to modify the Artist program given above. The modification consists of adding a module which takes the 20*3: grid contained in A$(1) and saving it on tape. This modification is left to you to accomplish and you will probably either choose to set aside a version of Artist which only creates and works with an array A$(20,30) and does not store colour characteristics or create a packed string, or you may choose to add to the existing Artist program which, with a simple loop such as FOR I = 1 TO 20: LET B$(I) = A$(1,I):NEXT I, transfers the content of A$(1) into another array.

In any event you must end up with a program which is capable of saving a 20*30 string containing a screenful of characters. The next step is to create some designs which reproduce the borders of a country and then store each one under the name of the country it represents. That is when we can take up the thread with this program.

MODULE 4.3.1

```
1000>REM ************************
1010 REM MENU
1020 REM ************************
1030 PRINT "                WHERE?"
1040 PRINT '"1)LOAD NEW COUNTRY"
1050 PRINT '"2)RECORD NEW CITIES
"
1060 PRINT '"3)SET QUESTIONS"
1070 PRINT '"4)INITIALISE"
1080 PRINT '"5)STOP"
1090 INPUT Z$: CLS : LET QTOTAL=
0: LET WRONG=0
```

```
1100 IF Z$="1" THEN GO SUB 1260
1110 IF Z$="2" THEN GO SUB 1320
1120 IF Z$="3" THEN LET COUNTRY=
FN A(): GO SUB 1670: GO SUB 1510
1130 IF Z$="5" THEN GO TO 1160
1140 IF Z$="4" THEN GO SUB 1190
1150 CLS : GO TO 1000
1160 PRINT AT 10,10;"WHERE?"
1170 INPUT "Have you entered any
 new data  that you wish to rec
ord? (Y/N)";Q$: IF Q$="Y" THEN S
AVE "WHERE?": PRINT "Rewind then
""ENTER"" to verify.": PAUSE 0:
VERIFY "WHERE?"
1180 STOP
```

This is a standard menu module.

MODULE 4.3.2

```
1190 REM *************************
1200 REM INITIALISE
1210 REM *************************
1220 DIM B$(10,20,30)
1230 LET COUNTRIES=0
1240 DEF FN A()=INT (RND*COUNTRI
ES+1)
1250 RETURN
```

The variables are initialised here.

Commentary

Line 1220. The strings containing the countries are stored in the array B$.

Line 1240. This function chooses a random country.

MODULE 4.3.3

```
1260 REM ***********************
1270 REM LOAD NEW COUNTRY
1280 REM ***********************
1290 INPUT "NAME FOR COUNTRY TO
BE LOADED? ";N$: INPUT "START TA
PE THEN ""ENTER""";Q$: LOAD N$ D
ATA A$()
1300 INPUT "NUMBER TO BE LOADED
AT:";PLACE
1310 LET COUNTRIES=COUNTRIES+1:
FOR I=1 TO 20: LET B$(PLACE,I)=A
$(I): NEXT I: RETURN
```

This module accepts a 20*30 array from tape under the relevant country name and places it into B$, the position being decided upon by the user.

Testing Module 4.3.3
Load a string and place it into B$: check in direct mode that it has been properly stored.

MODULE 4.3.4

```
1320 REM ***********************
1330 REM RECORD CITIES
1340 REM ***********************
1350 INPUT "NUMBER OF COUNTRY? "
;COUNTRY
1360 PRINT : FOR I=1 TO 20: PRIN
T PAPER 5; INK 2;TAB 1;B$(COUNTR
Y,I): NEXT I: LET X=1: LET Y=1:
LET T$="": GO TO 1430
1370 PRINT OVER 1; PAPER 8; INK
0;AT X,Y;"*": PAUSE 2: PRINT OVE
R 1; PAPER 8; INK 0;AT X,Y;"*"
1380 LET T$=INKEY$: IF T$="" THE
N GO TO 1370
1390 IF T$<"5" OR T$>"9" THEN GO
 TO 1370
```

```
1400 PRINT PAPER 5; INK 2;AT X,Y
;B$(COUNTRY,X,Y)
1410 LET X=X+(T$="6")-(T$="7"):
LET X=X+(X<1)-(X>20)
1420 LET Y=Y+(T$="8")-(T$="5"):
LET Y=Y+(Y<1)-(Y>30)
1430 PRINT INK 0;AT 0,0;"X=";X;"
  Y=";Y;"  ""9"" TO STOP": IF T$
<>"9" THEN GO TO 1370
1440 PRINT AT 5,0;"A TYPICAL DAT
A ENTRY LOOKS LIKE THIS:"'"5100
DATA 5,""TOYLAND"""'"5101 DATA "
"TOYTOWN"",6,12"
1450 PRINT AT 10,0;"RECORD CITY
NAME, X & Y IN DATA STATEMENT AF
TER ";5000+COUNTRY*100;"."
1460 PRINT '"INCREASE NUMBER IN
DATA STATEMENT AT ";5000+COUNTRY
*100;" BY 1."
1470 PRINT '"SECOND ITEM IN THAT
 LINE SHOULD BE THE COUNTRY NAME
."'"ANY KEY TO LIST RELEVANT DAT
A."
1480 PAUSE 0: LIST 5000+COUNTRY*
100: STOP
```

This module allows the user to move a cursor around the design until the co-ordinates of a city are established to the user's satisfaction. These co-ordinates may then be entered into a data statement at the end of the program.

Commentary

Line 1360. The relevant section of the array B$ is printed on the screen.

Lines 1370-1420. These are standard routines for moving a cursor around.

Line 1430. The co-ordinates of the cursor are displayed on the screen.

Lines 1440-1480. If the user stops the program, instructions are given for entering the co-ordinates into a data statement at the end of the program. The structure of the data statement is as follows:

1) The name of each country is stored in a data statement numbered 5000 + (100 times its number in B$). The name of the country is preceded on that data line by the number of its cities whose co-ordinates are registered.

2) The data relating to cities are stored in the line immediately following e.g. 5101,5102 in the form of single lines, each containing a city name, followed by the X and Y co-ordinates.

If the city is the first to be entered for a country that has just been loaded, the country must be recorded in the place indicated by the program. If it is not the first city, the item recording the number of cities must be increased and the new city entered on a line of its own. The program provides the user with the number of the correct lines to enter the data and two example lines. In use this is an extremely simple method of entering new items and it serves as another example of the savings that can be made in the complexity of programs if the user is trusted to do a little pre-packaging of the information the program has to work on. Without the use of data lines we should have to make provision for an array to hold the city names and co-ordinates, together with a method of sorting and a method of deletion.

Testing Module 4.3.4

You should now be able to move the cursor around and stop the program with the input of a '9', upon which you should be given instructions for the entry of the city co-ordinates into the data statement.

MODULE 4.3.5

```
1670 RESTORE (5000+100*COUNTRY):
 READ N,C$: LET CITY=INT (RND*N+
1): RESTORE (5000+100*COUNTRY+CI
TY): READ M$,X,Y: RETURN
```

This line reads the data for a country and city indicated by the variables COUNTRY and CITY. It is a good example of the flexibility of the RESTORE function on the Spectrum.

MODULE 4.3.6

```
1510 REM ************************
1520 REM WHICH CITY
1530 REM ************************
1540 CLS : PRINT INK 0;C$: FOR I
=1 TO 20: PRINT PAPER 5: INK 2;T
AB 1;B$(COUNTRY,I): NEXT I
1550 PRINT OVER 1: PAPER 8: INK
0: FLASH 1;AT X,Y;"*"
1560 FOR I=1 TO 3
1570 LET QTOTAL=QTOTAL+1: INPUT
"NAME OF THIS CITY? ";N$: IF N$=
M$ THEN GO TO 1620
1580 PRINT AT 0,0;"WRONG!
                    ": PAUSE 100:
 PRINT AT 0,0;C$;" ": LET WRONG=
WRONG+1: NEXT I
1590 PRINT AT 0,0;"THE CITY WAS:
";M$: INPUT """ENTER"" TO CONTIN
UE";Q$
1600 PRINT INK 2; PAPER 5; FLASH
 0;AT X,Y;B$(COUNTRY,X,Y)
1610 GO TO 1630
1620 PRINT AT 0,0;"";M$;"
 ": FOR I=1 TO 20: PRINT FLASH 1
; INK 2; PAPER 5;AT I,1;B$(COUNT
RY,I): PRINT INK 1;AT I,I;"RIGHT
!": NEXT I: PRINT OVER 1; FLASH
1;AT X,Y;"*"
1630 PRINT INK 0;AT 21,0;"QUESTI
ONS:";QTOTAL;" RIGHT:";QTOTAL-WR
ONG;" %:";(QTOTAL-WRONG)/QTOTAL*
100
1640 INPUT "ANOTHER GO? (Y/N)? "
;Q$: IF Q$="N" THEN RETURN
1650 INPUT "SAME COUNTRY? (Y/N)?
 ";Q$: IF Q$="N" THEN LET COUNTR
Y=FN A()
1660 GO SUB 1670: GO TO 1510
```

This module prints out a country, adds a marker at the position of a city and requests an input as to the city's name. On the basis of the answers so far given an assessment is printed of the user's performance so far.

Commentary
Line 1570. The name input is tested against the name picked up from the data. Note that three attempts at each city are allowed.

Line 1620. A simple visual reward is given if the user inputs the correct name.

Line 1650. Note the use of the function to determine a new country if the user wishes to change countries.

Testing Module 4.3.6
The program should now be capable of setting a test based on the data you have input.

Summary
It is possible to abuse data statements. Many people do so by employing them in programs where data has to be frequently changed or sorted in one way or another. In the right place, however, data statements can be both convenient and time saving, since data can be added or deleted without constant reshuffling of huge arrays. There can be no hard and fast rule but if a program is always requiring the user to be stopping to enter new data then the programmer is probably just avoiding the task of creating a program which can deal with the type of data required in the way it really needs.

Going Further
1) Could you enlarge the program so that it could print rivers or mountains and other physical features and request the name. Not easy but possible and it would look extremely impressive.
2) Can you think of other applications for this program? One that comes to mind is questions on the analysis of circuits for those learning electronics e.g. what is the current at the point marked by the flashing cursor?

CHAPTER 5

UTILITIES – a collection of miscellaneous routines

In this chapter we consider six very disparate programs under the rough heading of 'utilities', illustrating, if nothing else, the variety of applications you may choose for one-off programs to suit particular needs of your own. The six programs are:

1) Calculator, which is designed to make your Spectrum more useful when it comes to repetitive series of calculations.

2) Calories, a program which perhaps illustrates the author's own pre-occupations but which, nevertheless, is a convenient tool for those who need to watch their weight.

3) Graph, a general purpose graph-drawing program.

4) Renumber, a vital tool for your own programming, allowing you to tidy up those irregularly numbered programs.

5) Unifile II. We revisit Unifile and develop it so that it can accept data of irregular size and structure. It now becomes a far more powerful program.

6) Typist, a simple program which can teach you to touch type.

5.1 Calculator

It may seem strange to design a program to make calculations easier on a computer. After all, is the Spectrum not capable of accepting formulae in direct mode for one-off calculations or in the form of straightforward programs for regular calculations?

The answer is, of course, that the Spectrum can do both. But in-between the one-off calculation that can easily be typed in, and the specialist use that is regular enough to justify writing a special program, as with the financial programs in Chapter 2, is a wide range of needs where repetitive calculations have to be made which would be too tiresome to enter in direct mode and yet not sufficiently important to make a special program seem worthwhile. For such applications, we need a program which will allow a range of formulae and variables to be entered and easily altered and their results displayed.

Having started on such a project we may as well at the same time design the program so that the results of changing the value of variables can be compared in the manner of a 'what if' program like the budget program in Chapter 2.

To achieve this without having to constantly write new formulae into program lines we shall make use of two of Sinclair Basic's most attractive features: — its flexible string handling and its ability to evaluate a numerical expression stored in a string. Taken together, these two will allow us to perform tasks which would be quite impossible on many other machines whose price far exceeds that of the Spectrum.

MODULE 5.1.1

```
1000 REM ************************
1010 REM MENU
1020 REM ************************
1030 CLS : INK 0: PAPER 7: PRINT
 "            CALCULATOR"
1040 PRINT '"1)INITIALISE"
1050 PRINT '"2)PRINT TABLE"
1060 PRINT '"3)RESET TABLE"
1070 PRINT '"4)DEFINE VARIABLES"
1080 PRINT '"5)DEFINE LINES"
1090 PRINT '"6)DISPLAY COLUMN VA
RIABLES"
1100 PRINT '"7)STOP"
1110 INPUT Z$: CLS
1120 IF Z$="1" THEN GO SUB 1220
1130 IF Z$="2" THEN GO SUB 1300
1140 IF Z$="3" THEN GO SUB 1400
1150 IF Z$="4" THEN GO SUB 1690
1160 IF Z$="5" THEN GO SUB 1810
1170 IF Z$="6" THEN GO SUB 1920
1180 IF Z$="7" THEN GO TO 1200
1190 CLS : GO TO 1030
1200 PRINT AT 10,10;"CALCULATOR"
: INPUT "HAVE YOU ENTERED NEW DA
TA YOU   WISH TO SAVE? (Y/N) ";Q
$: IF Q$="Y" THEN SAVE "CALCULAT
OR": BEEP 1,40: PRINT "REWIND TH
EN ANY KEY TO VERIFY.": PAUSE 0:
```

```
 VERIFY "CALCULATOR": PRINT "VER
IFIED"
1210 STOP
```

Another standard menu module.

MODULE 5.1.2

```
1220 REM ************************
1230 REM INITIALISE
1240 REM ************************
1250 DIM A$(20,10): DIM B$(20,10
): DIM C$(20,50): DIM E$(20,50)
1260 DIM B(20,10): DIM D(20,10)
1270 LET LINES=0: LET VARIABLES=
0
1290 RETURN
```

The use of the various arrays will be explained in the course of the program.

MODULE 5.1.3

```
1690 REM ************************
1700 REM DEFINE VARIABLES
1710 REM ************************
1720 CLS : FOR I=1 TO VARIABLES:
 PRINT I;") ";B$(I): NEXT I
1730 INPUT "1)EXISTING   2)NEW
 3)QUIT ";Q$: IF Q$="3" THEN RET
URN
1740 IF Q$="1" THEN INPUT "NUMBE
R? ";N: GO TO 1760
1750 IF Q$="2" THEN INPUT "VARIA
BLE NAME? ";N$: LET VARIABLES=VA
RIABLES+1: LET N=VARIABLES: LET
B$(VARIABLES)=N$
1760 CLS : PRINT B$(N): FOR I=1
TO 10: PRINT I;") ";B(N,I): NEXT
 I
```

```
1770 INPUT "NUMBER_""ZZZ"" QUIT_
""DDD"" DELETE  ";Q$: IF Q$="ZZZ
" THEN GO TO 1720
1780 IF Q$="DDD" THEN FOR I=N TO
 VARIABLES-1: LET B$(I)=B$(I+1):
 FOR J=1 TO 10: LET B(I,J)=B(I+1
,J): NEXT J: NEXT I: LET B$(VARI
ABLES)="": FOR I=1 TO 10: LET B(
VARIABLES,I)=0: NEXT I: LET VARI
ABLES=VARIABLES-1: RETURN
1790 INPUT "VALUE? (""X"" EQUAL
TO COLUMN ONE) ";N$: IF N$="X" T
HEN LET B(N,VAL Q$)=B(N,1): GO T
O 1760
1800 LET B(N,VAL Q$)=VAL N$: GO
TO 1760
```

The purpose of this module is to allow the user to name up to 20 different variables and to specify a series of 10 values for each variable named, thus allowing comparative calculations to be easily made.

Commentary

Lines 1720-1730. The names of the variables so far defined are stored in the array B$ and are displayed on entry to this module.

Line 1750. New variable names are placed into the array in a position defined by the variable VARIABLES, which is set at zero to begin with and is incremented for each new name.

Line 1760. The 10 values associated with the specified variables are stored in the array B. These are displayed so that the user may specify changes.

Testing Module 5.1.3

The variables specified are of no practical use at this point but the module should be capable of accepting up to 20 names, together with 10 associated values and of deleting names and values.

MODULE 5.1.4

```
1920 REM ************************
1930 REM DISPLAY COLUMN
1940 REM ************************
1950 CLS : INPUT "WHICH COLUMN?
(0 TO QUIT) ";N: IF N=0 THEN RET
URN
1960 CLS : PRINT "COLUMN ";N
1970 FOR I=1 TO VARIABLES: PRINT
 I;") ";B$(I);" ";B(I,N): NEXT I
1980 INPUT "NUMBER FOR AMENDMENT
 ""ZZZ"" QUIT";Q$: IF Q$="ZZZ" T
HEN GO TO 1950
1990 INPUT "NEW VALUE FOR VARIAB
LE? ";R: LET B(VAL Q$,N)=R: GO T
O 1960
```

The previous module allowed the display of all the values associated with a single variable. This module displays the first, second or nth value associated with each variable. Thus, if a series of calculations are to be performed on a series of years' data, this module would display the value of each variable for one particular year.

Testing Module 5.1.4
If you have named some variables and input some values for them you should be able to display a column of them.

MODULE 5.1.5

```
1810 REM ************************
1820 REM DEFINE LINES
1830 REM ************************
1840 CLS : PRINT "            LI
NES"
1850 FOR I=1 TO LINES: PRINT I;"
)";" "+A$(I)+" ";C$(I): NEXT I
1860 INPUT "1)EXISTING    2)NEW
 3)DELETE    4)QUIT";Q$: IF Q$="4
" THEN RETURN
```

```
1870 IF Q$="2" THEN INPUT "LINE
TITLE? ";N$: LET LINES=LINES+1:
LET N=LINES: LET A$(LINES)=N$: I
NPUT "FORMULA? ";F$: LET C$(LINE
S)=F$: GO SUB 1490: LET E$(N)=G$
: GO TO 1840
1880 IF Q$="1" THEN INPUT "NUMBE
R? ";N: INPUT "NEW TITLE? (Y/N)
";T$: IF T$="Y" THEN INPUT "SPEC
IFY NEW TITLE: ";T$: LET A$(N)=T
$
1890 IF Q$="1" THEN INPUT "NEW F
ORMULA? (Y/N) ";T$: IF T$="Y" TH
EN INPUT "SPECIFY NEW FORMULA: "
;F$: LET C$(N)=F$: GO SUB 1490:
LET E$(N)=G$: GO TO 1840
1900 IF Q$="3" THEN INPUT "NUMBE
R? ";N: FOR I=N TO LINES-1: LET
A$(I)=A$(I+1): LET C$(I)=C$(I+1)
: NEXT I: LET A$(LINES)="": LET
C$(LINES)="": LET LINES=LINES-1
1910 RETURN
```

In order to understand this module you need to know a little about the ability of the Spectrum to evaluate an expression stored in a string. This seems, at first sight, an unimportant capability. What on earth is the use of being able to instruct the Spectrum to PRINT VAL '1 + 1' — or any other expression for that matter — when it can be done more simply with PRINT 1 + 1. The answer is that while a straight numerical expression like 1 + 1 can only be incorporated into a program line, '1 + 1' can be placed into a program line or stored and manipulated like any other string. This module takes advantage of that fact to store formulae input by the user.

Commentary
Line 1850. The number of formulae so far input is stored in the variable LINES. The formulae, in the form input by the user, are stored in the array A$ which limits the length of each to 50 characters.

Line 1870. The formula, which may be up to 50 characters long as previously noted, can be anything which the Spectrum would recognise as having a value. The only limit is that variable names may not contain numbers. Thus AA would be recognised as a variable name, while A1 would not. The only exception to this is that one formula can use the results of another by including a variable such as LINE1 + 10, this would be evaluated as the result of the first formula input plus 10.

Testing Module 5.1.5
This module cannot be tested fully until the next two have been entered. If a temporary line 1490 LET G$ = F$:RETURN is entered, the module should accept formulae, together with brief identifying titles up to 10 characters and should allow changes and deletions.

MODULE 5.1.6

```
1490 REM ************************
1500 REM IDENTIFY VARIABLES
1510 REM ************************
1520 LET G$="": LET V$=""
1530 FOR I=1 TO LEN F$: IF F$(I)
=" " THEN GO TO 1610
1540 IF F$(I)>="A" AND F$(I)<="Z
" THEN LET V$=V$+F$(I): GO TO 16
00
1550 IF LEN V$>=4 THEN IF V$(1 TO
4)="LINE" AND (F$(I)> ="0" AND F
$(I)<="9") THEN LET V$ =V$+F$(I)
: GO TO 1600
1560 IF LEN V$>=4 THEN IF V$(1 TO
4)="LINE" AND LEN V$= 4 AND ((F$
(I)<"0" OR F$(I)>"Z") OR (F$(I)<
"A" AND F$(I)>"9")) TH EN PRINT
"LINE  UNDEFINED":  PAUSE  200:
RETURN
1570 IF LEN V$>=4 THEN  IF V$(1
TO 4)="LINE" AND (F$(I)<  "A" OR
F$(I)>"Z")  THEN GO SUB 16  30:
LET V$="": LET G$=G$+F$(I):GO TO
1600
1580 IF V$<>"" AND (F$(I)<"A" OR
 F$(I)>"Z") THEN GO SUB 1630: LE
T G$=G$+F$(I): LET V$="": GO TO
1600
1590 LET G$=G$+F$(I)
```

```
1600 NEXT I
1610 IF LEN V$>0 THEN GO SUB 163
0
1620 RETURN
```

Having input something which is recognisable to the Spectrum as a formula we run up against a problem — that of giving a value to the variables that the formula contains. If the formula were to contain a variable by the name of STOTAL, a valid name for the program, the value of the formula could still not be extracted unless the Spectrum had a value for that variable, something that can only be done using an INPUT or a LET statement. e.g. LET STOTAL=10.

It would be difficult to call such a procedure flexible and easy to use compared with the way in which variables were named and given values in Module 3. The fact is that while the items stored in B$ may be called variables for the purpose of the program, they are nothing of the kind to the Spectrum itself and would not be recognised if they were included in a formula to be evaluated. The variable names input by the user are never used in the calculations performed by this program. They are replaced by other variable names for which the Spectrum does have an accompanying value.

In this module, and the next, the formula input by the user is translated into terms which the Spectrum can handle. It has already been noted that up to 10 values can be input alongside a named variable and that these 10 values are stored in the array B. Thus, to the Spectrum, each of these values has a name of the FORM B(X,Y), where X is the number of the associated variable name in B$ and Y is the column number from 1 to 10. These two modules create a new formula to replace that input by the user, whose variables will be elements taken from the array B. The Spectrum can be asked to evaluate this second formula using the VAL function since all its variables are defined. Thus a user input formula such as CIRCLES*PI*RADIUS↑2 would become something like B(1,3)*PI*B(2,3)↑2.

Commentary
Line 1520. G$ will be used to store the translated formula as it is built up, ultimately it will be stored in the array E$ parallel to the position of its parent formula in A$. V$ is used to temporarily store names identified in the user input formula.

Line 1530. The user-defined formula will be stored in an array line of 50 characters and will usually not fill that space. The module considers the formula to be at an end when it encounters the first empty space.

Line 1540. If a character encountered in the user defined formula falls in the range A-Z then it is taken as part of a variable name and added to whatever is in V$.

Line 1550. The first statement in this line may strike you as a little odd; it is in fact needed to avoid an error message if V$ is less than four characters long and a condition such as IF V$(1 TO 4) = "LINE" is specified. If V$ is less than four characters long this line is not executed and if V$ is four or more characters long, the statement makes absolutely no difference to the execution of the program — an interesting use of the way the Spectrum defaults on encountering a false condition. The purpose of the main part of the line is to make a special provision for recognising variables of the form LINE1, LINE2 etc which were mentioned earlier.

Line 1560. This line simply checks that if a variable begins with the letters LINE, it has an identifying number to follow.

Line 1570. This line recognises when a LINE variable is complete by identifying the first character that cannot be contained within such a variable.

Line 1580. Returning to the normal type of variable name, which will contain only letters, this line recognises when such a variable is complete.

Line 1590. Characters which are not part of a variable name are simply added to the translated formula.

Line 1610. Normally, the completion of a variable name is recognised because:
A) V$ contains some characters
B) The next character encountered could not be part of a variable.

Clearly this cannot work if the variable name is at the end of the formula which is why this line is used to check whether V$, which is emptied after each successful identification, contained anything.

Testing Module 5.1.6
This can only be accomplished after the entry of the next short module.

MODULE 5.1.7

```
1630 REM ************************
1640 REM EVALUATE
1650 REM ************************
1660 IF LEN V$>=4 THEN  IF V$(1
TO 4)="LINE" THEN LET G$  =G$+"D
("+V$(5 TO )+",J)": RETURN
1670 FOR J=1 TO VARIABLES: IF V$
<>B$(J,1 TO LEN V$) THEN NEXT J:
 PRINT "VARIABLE ";V$;" NOT FOUN
D.": PAUSE 200: LET IND=0: RETUR
N
1680 LET G$=G$+"B("+STR$ J+",J)"
: RETURN
```

The previous module having identified names in the user-defined formula, this module translates such names into terms the Spectrum can handle in calculations.

Commentary
Line 1660. The results of evaluations of formulae will be placed into the array D at a later point. This line translates a variable name such as LINE3 into the name of an element in D, such as D(3,J). 'J' is used because at a later point the stored formulae will be evaluated by two loops, an I loop referring to the number of formulae and a J loop referring to each of the 10 possible values for each variable
Line 1670. For an ordinary variable, this line checks through the existing variable names and informs the user if no such variable has been defined.

Line 1680. If the variable name has already been declared, the relevant element from the array B is added to G$. If the variable STOTAL were third in the list of variables, it would be translated as B(3,J).

Testing Module 5.1.7
You should now be able to input the variable names and specify a series of values for each. Input a formula composed of numbers, mathematical symbols and variables which you have defined. Stop the program and check that this has been sensibly translated. You should find it stored in the temporary string G$ and as an element in the array E$. If you know the correct answer to your particular formula you can test the accuracy of the modules by entering PRINT VAL G$ in

direct mode. You should also be able to use the results of one formula as a variable in another, using LINE variables.

MODULE 5.1.8

```
1400 REM ************************
1410 REM RESET TABLE
1420 REM ************************
1430 INPUT "HOW MANY COLUMNS? ";
COLUMNS
1440 FOR K=1 TO LINES: LET F$=C$
(K): GO SUB 1490: LET E$(K)=G$:
NEXT K
1450 FOR I=1 TO LINES: FOR J=1 T
O COLUMNS
1460 LET D(I,J)=VAL E$(I)
1470 NEXT J: NEXT I
1480 RETURN
```

Once having evaluated the results of the user-defined formulae using the range of values specified for the named variables, you may wish to alter a particular variable. Rather than re-evaluate everything every time a variable is altered, this module re-calculates the whole table of 'lines and columns' when the user specifies. Untranslated formulae are called up from the array C$ and re-translated on the basis of the latest data.

Commentary
Line 1460. It may appear at first sight that this line sets a whole series of elements in the array D to the same value but this is not so. The evaluation of E$(I) will alter with every change in J, since we have already translated the user-defined variables into the form B(X,J) or D(X,J). Note that no attempt is made to deal with the problems raised by interaction of the values of LINEs. If the value of LINE1 depends upon the value of LINE2, and LINE2 is to be altered by this loop, the value of LINE1 will not take account of that fact unless the module is called twice. More complex interactions between the lines should be thought out before they are entered.

MODULE 5.1.9

```
1300 REM ************************
1310 REM PRINT TABLE
1320 REM ************************
1330 INPUT "COLUMN FOR DISPLAY?
(0=QUIT)";COLUMN: PAPER 7: IF CO
LUMN=0 THEN PAPER 7: RETURN
1340 CLS : PRINT "LINES      FIG
URES"
1350 FOR I=1 TO LINES: PAPER (5+
2*(I/2=INT (I/2))): PRINT A$(I);
" ";
1360 LET M$=STR$ D(I,COLUMN): IF
 LEN M$>10 THEN PRINT M$( TO 10)
: GO TO 1380
1370 PRINT M$
1380 NEXT I
1390 GO TO 1330
```

This module prints out the brief title of each line or formula and the value derived from the line when based on one of the 10 possible columns of variable values.

Commentary

Lines 1360-1370. These two lines truncate any figure to 10 digits. The only purpose of this is to allow two columns to be displayed with minimal changes to the program. If you are likely to have 10 digits or more regularly, you may wish to alter this.

Testing Module 5.1.9

You should now be able to fully test the program by inputting up to 20 variables, each with 10 possible values, up to 20 lines of formulae using these variables and brief titles to each of these lines and display the results, column by column. If these tests are satisfactory the program is ready for use.

Summary

As general purpose programs go, this one seems unexciting at first glance. It can, however, be highly useful in a wide variety of fields. In business it can be used to examine the effects of changes in the cost of materials or in prices or in both. At home it can be an adjunct to the financial programs in chapter 2, performing each calculation for tax, if you can work out the relevant formula. Hobbyists may wish to use it for repetitive calculations in other fields. Like many of the programs in this book it is a flexible tool and you will only gain a proper insight into its capabilities by playing with it, applying it and altering it to your own needs.

Going Further

1) If you do not need more than three or four digits for some applications, adapt the program so that it can display several columns at once.

2) If you own a 48K Spectrum, extend the program to cover more variables and formulae thus providing the opportunity to build up a library of useful formulae.

5.2 Calories

As it stands this program may or may not be useful to you. If you need to count the calories then it can save you a lot of time and make your efforts that much more accurate. Whether or not you are interested in calories this program bears careful study as an example of the way in which the modular style of programming we have adopted allows previously written material to be quickly adapted for other uses. This program is a thinly disguised copy of large sections of MultiQ. The brevity of the comments on the program will give you some idea of the speed with which it was written. Despite that fact it is an important program in the sense that it shows how dictionaries of items and related quantities can be built up and used.

MODULE 5.2.1

```
1180 REM ************************
1190 REM MENU
1200 REM ************************
1210 BORDER 4: INK 0: PAPER 7: C
LS : PRINT "                MENU"
1220 PRINT '"1)DISPLAY TODAY'S L
IST"
1230 PRINT '"2)INPUT TO TODAY'S
LIST"
1240 PRINT '"3)START FRESH LIST"
1250 PRINT '"4)DELETE FROM DAY'S
 LIST"
1260 PRINT '"5)EXTEND DICTIONARY
"
1270 PRINT '"6)DISPLAY DICTIONAR
Y/DELETE"
1280 PRINT '"7)INITIALISE"
1290 PRINT '"8)STOP"
1300 INPUT "Which do you require
?";Z$: CLS
```

```
1310 IF Z$="1" THEN GO SUB 1430
1320 IF Z$="2" THEN GO SUB 1580
1330 IF Z$="3" THEN GO SUB 1700
1340 IF Z$="4" THEN GO SUB 2520
1350 IF Z$="5" THEN GO SUB 1740
1360 IF Z$="6" THEN GO SUB 2170
1370 IF Z$="7" THEN GO TO 1030
1380 IF Z$="8" THEN GO TO 1400
1390 CLS : GO TO 1180
1400 PRINT FLASH 1;AT 10,12;"CAL
ORIES"
1410 INPUT "HAVE YOU INPUT NEW I
NFORMATION  YOU WISH TO SAVE? (Y
/N)";Q$: IF Q$="Y" THEN SAVE "CA
LORIES": BEEP 1,40: PRINT '"REWI
ND, THEN ANY KEY TO VERIFY": PAU
SE 0: VERIFY "CALORIES": PRINT '
"VERIFIED"
1420 STOP
```

A standard menu module.

MODULE 5.2.2

```
   1 GO TO 1180
1000 REM ************************
1010 REM VARIABLES
1020 REM ************************
1030 DIM A$(500,15)
1040 DIM B$(500,15)
1050 DIM C(500)
1060 DIM T$(50,2,20)
1070 DIM O$(32)
1080 DIM T(50)
1090 LET LIST=0
```

```
1100 LET ENDITEM=3
1110 LET ITEMS=2
1120 LET I$=CHR$ 0+CHR$ 1+CHR$ 0
+CHR$ 2
1130 LET A$(2,1)=CHR$ 255
1140 LET P$="    "
1150 DIM F$(15)
1160 DIM G$(17)
1170 LET L$="*******************
**************"
```

Why did I put the variables before the menu? Well, it seemed like a good idea at the time. The use of the various arrays will be discussed during the course of the program.

MODULE 5.2.3

```
1740 REM ***********************
1750 REM INPUT ITEMS
1760 REM ***********************
1770 CLS : PRINT "   NEW ITEMS F
OR DICTIONARY"
1780 PRINT '"FOOD:": INPUT "NAME
 OR ""ZZZ"" TO QUIT";F$: IF F$(
TO 3)="ZZZ" THEN RETURN
1790 PRINT AT 2,5;F$
1800 PRINT '"UNITS:": INPUT "NAM
E ";G$
1810 PRINT AT 4,6;G$
1820 PRINT '"CALORIES PER UNIT:"
: INPUT "NAME ";H$
1830 LET TEMP=VAL H$
1840 PRINT AT 6,18;H$
1850 INPUT "Are these correct? (
Y/N)";Q$: IF Q$="N" THEN GO TO 1
770
1860 CLS : GO SUB 1880: GO SUB 2
030
1870 LET ITEMS=ITEMS+1: GO TO 17
40
```

This straightforward module accepts three inputs representing the name of a food, the units in which it is habitually measured and the number of calories per unit.

MODULE 5.2.4

```
1880 REM *************************
1890 REM BINARY SEARCH
1900 REM *************************
1910 DEF FN A()=256*CODE I$(2*S-
1)+CODE I$(2*S)
1920 LET POWER=INT (LN (ITEMS)/L
N 2)
1930 LET S=2^POWER
1940 FOR I=POWER-1 TO 0 STEP -1
1950 LET P=FN A()
1960 LET S=S-(2^I)*(A$(P)>F$)+(2
^I)*(A$(P)<F$)
1970 IF S<2 THEN LET S=2
1980 IF S>ITEMS-1 THEN LET S=ITE
MS-1
1990 NEXT I
2000 LET P=FN A()
2010 IF A$(P)>F$ THEN LET S=S-1
2020 RETURN
```

This is a straight binary search to determine the place of the food in the overall dictionary of foods stored in A$. Up to 500 foods can be stored, each with a name of up to 15 characters in length.

MODULE 5.2.5

```
2030 REM *************************
2040 REM INSERTION
2050 REM *************************
2060 IF LEN P$=4 THEN GO TO 2100
2070 LET PLACE=256*CODE P$(3)+CO
DE P$(4)
2080 LET P$=P$( TO 2)+P$(5 TO )
2090 GO TO 2120
2100 LET PLACE=ENDITEM
```

```
2110 LET ENDITEM=ENDITEM+1
2120 LET A$(PLACE)=F$
2130 LET B$(PLACE)=G$
2140 LET C(PLACE)=TEMP
2150 LET I$=I$( TO 2*S)+CHR$ INT
 (PLACE/256)+CHR$ INT (PLACE-256
*INT (PLACE/256))+I$(2*S+1 TO )
2160 RETURN
```

This module inserts the new item into the correct place in the order using the method outlined in MultiQ. Empty spaces in the list are filled first, followed by the positions at the end of the list. The true order is indicated by character pairs in the pointer array, I$.

Testing Module 5.2.5

At this point, although the dictionary cannot easily be displayed, you should be capable of entering items into the dictionary. These will be stored in A$ in the order in which they were input. Associated units and calorific values should be stored in the parallel positions in B$ and C respectively. The correct order of items should be discernable from the code value of character pairs in I$.

MODULE 5.2.6

```
2170 REM ***********************
2180 REM USER SEARCH
2190 REM ***********************
2200 PRINT "              DISPLA
Y"
2210 PRINT '"ON APPEARANCE OF IT
EM, INPUT:"
2220 PRINT '">POSITIVE OR NEGATI
VE NUMBER TO MOVE POINTER"
2230 PRINT '">""DDD"" TO DELETE
ITEM"
2240 PRINT '">""ZZZ"" TO QUIT FU
NCTION"
2250 PRINT L$
2260 IF ITEMS=2 THEN RETURN
2270 LET S=2
```

```
2280 LET P=FN A( )
2290 PRINT AT 12,0;"ENTRY No. ";
S-1
2300 PRINT '"FOOD:";A$(P)
2310 PRINT '"UNITS:";B$(P)
2320 PRINT '"CALORIES:";C(P);"
"
2330 INPUT "Which do you require
?";S$
2340 IF S$="DDD" THEN GO SUB 244
0: RETURN
2350 IF S$="ZZZ" THEN RETURN
2360 IF S$<>"" THEN GO TO 2400
2370 LET S=S+1
2380 IF S=ITEMS THEN RETURN
2390 GO TO 2280
2400 LET S=S+VAL S$
2410 IF S>=ITEMS THEN RETURN
2420 IF S<2 THEN LET S=2
2430 GO TO 2280
```

This is a simple search module based on that used in MultiQ. There is no true search; the user can simply page backwards and forwards. The deletion module is also called up by this module.

Testing Module 5.2.6
You should now be able to display all the foods input on command.

MODULE 5.2.7

```
2440 REM ************************
2450 REM DELETIONS
2460 REM ************************
2470 LET P=FN A( ): LET A$(P)="":
 LET B$(P)="": LET C(P)=0
2480 LET I$=I$( TO 2*S-2)+I$(2*S
```

```
+1 TO )
2490 LET ITEMS=ITEMS-1
2500 LET P$=P$( TO 2)+CHR$ INT (
P/256)+CHR$ INT (P-256*INT (P/25
6))+P$(3 TO )
2510 RETURN
```

This is the deletion method used in MultiQ. The address of the deleted item is removed from I$ and the space it leaves is recorded in P$. Note that the entry is not actually removed at any point from the array. The program is simply no longer aware of it.

Testing Module 5.2.7
You should now be able to delete items from the dictionary.

MODULE 5.2.8

```
1580 REM ************************
1590 REM ADD TO TODAY'S LIST
1600 REM ************************
1610 PRINT "       ADD TO TODAY'S
LIST"
1620 PRINT '"FOOD:": INPUT F$: P
RINT AT 2,5;F$
1630 GO SUB 1880: IF A$(P)<>F$ T
HEN PRINT AT 10,0;"*SPECIFIED  F
OOD UNKNOWN, PLEASE CHECK.": PAU
SE 200: RETURN
1640 PRINT '"UNITS:";B$(P)
1650 PRINT '"QUANTITY:": INPUT Q
: PRINT AT 6,9;Q
1660 INPUT "Are these correct? (
Y/N)";Q$: CLS : IF Q$="N" THEN G
O TO 1580
1670 LET LIST=LIST+1: LET T$(LIS
T,1)=A$(P): LET T$(LIST,2)=STR$
Q+" "+B$(P): LET T(LIST)=Q*C(P)
1680 INPUT "Any more items? (Y/N
)";Q$: CLS : IF Q$="Y" THEN GO T
O 1580
1690 RETURN
```

With this module we depart from the framework taken from MultiQ and come to the parts unique to our new application. The purpose of this module is to allow a daily list of foods to be quickly created, based on food already contained within the dictionary. The list does not have to be made up at one time but as foods are eaten or menus planned.

Line 1630. Note the interesting use of the binary search module here. When a food is input for the daily list, the name is sent to the search module which identifies the position that the food would hold if it were contained in the dictionary. On return from the search the food at that position is compared with the food input for the daily list. If they are not the same then the food input for the daily list is not contained in the dictionary and the user is informed. The use of RANDOMIZE in statement 2 is simply a means of defaulting if the food is found in the dictionary.

Line 1670. The current daily list is stored in two halves of the array T$ and the associated calorific values in T.

Testing Module 5.2.8
The program should now accept the input of foods to the daily list, display the usual units of measurements and invite an input for quantity. Foods not present in the dictionary will not be accepted.

MODULE 5.2.9

```
1430 REM *************************
1440 REM TODAY'S LIST
1450 REM *************************
1460 LET TOTAL=0
1470 FOR I=1 TO LIST
1480 PRINT "FOOD      :";T$(I,1)
1490 PRINT "AMOUNT    :";T$(I,2)
1500 PRINT "CALORIES:";T(I)
1510 PRINT L$
1520 LET TOTAL=TOTAL+T(I)
1530 NEXT I
1540 PRINT '"TOTAL CALORIES:";TO
TAL
1550 PRINT '"Press any key to co
ntinue."
1560 PAUSE 0
1570 RETURN
```

This module simply displays the list of foods for the day, giving their name, the amount and the total calories for the amount. At the end of the list the total calories for the list are displayed.

MODULE 5.2.10

```
1700 REM ************************
1710 REM NEW LIST
1720 REM ************************
1730 DIM T$(50,2,20): DIM T(50):
 LET LIST=0: GO SUB 1580: RETURN
```

This module allows the arrays relating to the daily list to be initialised without affecting the main arrays.

MODULE 5.2.11

```
2520 REM ************************
2530 REM DELETE FROM LIST
2540 REM ************************
2550 FOR I=1 TO LIST
2560 PRINT T$(I,1)
2570 INPUT "DDD=DELETE/ENTER=NEX
T/ZZZ=QUIT";Q$: IF Q$="ZZZ" THEN
 RETURN
2580 IF Q$="DDD" THEN GO TO 2600
2590 NEXT I: RETURN
2600 LET T$(I,1)="": LET T$(I,2)
="": LET T(I)=0
2610 FOR J=I TO LIST-1
2620 LET T$(J,1)=T$(J+1,1)
2630 LET T$(J,2)=T$(J+1,2)
2640 LET T(J)=T(J+1)
2650 NEXT J
2660 LET LIST=LIST-1
2670 RETURN
```

This module deletes items from the daily list.

Testing Module 5.2.11
You should now be able to set up a daily list, display it and delete from it. You should also be able to initialise the arrays to start a fresh list. If these tests are satisfactory the program is ready for use.

Summary
I hope that during the course of this program you have come to realise the advantage of the modular approach to program writing. It allowed the greater part of this program simply to be lifted from a very different application. As time goes by and you have developed your own favourite methods of dealing with different kinds of materials and processes you will develop an eye for ways of achieving a new application of your Spectrum using methods you already understand and program lines you have already tested and debugged.

From this you must draw the important lesson that it is more important to gather methods than programs, though programs may also often contain new methods. A good library of programs will stand you in good stead until a new application comes along. A good collection of methods, contained in working modules, is a useful background no matter what you want to accomplish. Do scan the books and magazines on the market for new ways to accomplish tasks and, when you find a good one, incorporate it into a working program even if it's not actually vital. It will be ready for that rainy day.

In the midst of all these generalisations do not lose sight of the fact that this program has a wide range of potential applications. Food is by no means the only area where it is useful to have a dictionary of items associated with their typical units and a value of some kind. Shopkeepers, for instance, usually stock less than 500 lines, each sold in a unit of some kind at a price. Why not adapt the program for some such use? Remember that it is methods that count rather than programs. This program is a working example of a method, if you see what I mean.....

Going Further
1) One major difference between this program and MultiQ is that MultiQ dimensioned its own arrays to cope with a variety of applications while using memory to the fullest. Could you change the program so that it became a general purpose name and quantity tool, with the names of the items specified by the user.

5.3 Graph
This short program is a general purpose graph drawer which allows the user to define the units on both axes in terms of both name and length and to input data in or out of order to create a line graph.

MODULE 5.3.1

```
1000 REM ************************
1010 REM MENU
1020 REM ************************
1030 CLS : PRINT AT 0,12; FLASH
1; INK 2;"GRAPH"
1040 PRINT '"1)SET UP FRAMEWORK"
1050 PRINT '"2)INPUT VALUES"
1060 PRINT '"3)DRAW GRAPH"
1070 PRINT '"4)INITIALISE"
1080 PRINT '"5)STOP"
1090 INPUT Z$: CLS
1100 IF Z$="1" THEN GO SUB 1180
1110 IF Z$="2" THEN GO SUB 1350
1120 IF Z$="3" THEN GO SUB 1530
1130 IF Z$="4" THEN CLEAR : LET
Z$="1"
1140 IF Z$="5" THEN GO TO 1160
1150 GO TO 1000
1160 PRINT AT 10,12; FLASH 1; IN
K 2;"GRAPH": INPUT "DO YOU WISH
TO RECORD?";Q$: IF Q$="Y" THEN S
AVE "GRAPH": INPUT "REWIND, THEN
 ""ENTER"" TO VERIFY.";Q$: VERIF
Y "GRAPH": PRINT '"     PROGRAM
VERIFIED."
1170 STOP
```

Another standard menu module. Note line 1130: Z$ needs to be set to '1' after the memory is CLEARed or an error message will be generated at line 1140 since there will be no Z$.

MODULE 5.3.2

```
1180 REM ************************
1190 REM SET UP AXES
1200 REM ************************
1210 PRINT "HOW MANY INTERVALS O
N THE          HORIZONTAL AXIS? ";:
 INPUT H: PRINT H: LET LH=INT (2
36/H)
1220 PRINT "HOW MANY INTERVALS O
N THE          VERTICAL ACCESS? ";:
 INPUT V: PRINT V: LET LV=INT (1
56/V)
1230 CLS : PRINT AT 8,3; FLASH 1
; INK 2;"AXES WILL LOOK LIKE THI
S"
1240 LET VMARK=300: LET HMARK=30
0: GO SUB 1450
1250 INPUT "YOU CAN SET A MARKER
 EVERY SO    MANY SPACES.
             INPUT GAP FOR HORIZ.
:";HMARK
1260 INPUT "GAP FOR VERTICAL:";V
MARK
1270 CLS : GO SUB 1450
1280 INPUT "IS THAT SATISFACTORY
? (Y/N)";Q$: IF Q$="N" THEN CLS
: GO TO 1180
1290 INPUT "NAME OF HORIZ. UNITS
? ";H$
1300 INPUT "NAME OF VERT. UNITS?
 ";V$
1310 PRINT '"MIN. VALUE ON V. AX
IS? ": INPUT BASE
1320 PRINT "MAX. VALUE REPRESENT
ED BY ";V'"UNITS? ": INPUT LIMIT
1330 LET VVAL=(LIMIT-BASE)/V
1340 DIM G(H): FOR I=1 TO H: LET
 G(I)=-999: NEXT I: RETURN
```

The purpose of this module is to allow the user to specify how many intervals there will be on the horizontal and vertical axes and to name the units involved.

Commentary

Line 1210. The horizontal axis will be 236 pixels long. The variable LH (length horizontal) is set to 236 divided by the desired number of intervals. This will usually result in there being slightly more intervals than the user has specified.

Line 1220. A similar variable is created for the vertical axis.

Lines 1240-1280. Units will be marked on the axes by small DRAWn lines. As an aid to clarity some of the lines can be slightly longer e.g. Every fifth unit can highlighted. The intervals at which this will occur are stored in HMARK and VMARK. These are set to 300 when the axes are first drawn, so that no marks are highlighted on either axis. When the basic axes have been displayed the user is invited to specify the intervals for these highlights and the axes are re-displayed for confirmation.

Lines 1290-1320. The names of the units on both axes are requested. It is assumed that the units on the horizontal axis start from zero but for the vertical axis the user is asked to specify the value at which the axis starts and the value at which it ends. From this is calculated the value of an individual unit on the vertical axis, this being kept in the variable VVAL. Units on the horizontal axis are assumed to have a value of 1.

Line 1340. The array G is dimensioned ready for the possible H items of data.

Testing Module 5.3.2

The axes cannot be drawn until the next module has been entered but by inserting a temporary line 1450 RETURN. The module should be able to request the number of intervals, the highlighting mark and the name of the units.

MODULE 5.3.3

```
1450 REM ************************
1460 REM DRAW AXES
1470 REM ************************
1480 FOR I=1 TO 19: PRINT AT I,1
;"▌": NEXT I: PRINT AT 20,1;"▙";
1490 FOR I=1 TO 29: PRINT "▄";:
NEXT I
1500 LET C=0: FOR I=11+LH TO 247
 STEP LH: LET C=C+1: PLOT INVERS
E 1; OVER 1;I,13: DRAW OVER 1;0,
-5-3*(C/HMARK=INT (C/HMARK)): NE
XT I
```

```
1510 LET C=0: FOR I=11+LV TO 167
 STEP LV: LET C=C+1: PLOT INVERS
E 1; OVER 1;13,I: DRAW OVER 1;-5
-3*(C/VMARK=INT (C/VMARK)),0: NE
XT I
1520 RETURN
```

This module draws the axes for the graph.

Commentary

Line 1500. The horizontal axis is filled with intersecting lines five pixels long and LH pixels apart. At every HMARK interval, the line is three pixels longer.

Line 1510. A similar process is repeated for the vertical axis.

Testing Module 5.3.3

You should now be able to input details of units and unit names and have the axes displayed for confirmation.

MODULE 5.3.4

```
1350 REM ************************
1360 REM INPUT VALUES
1370 REM ************************
1380 PRINT "NUMBER OF ";H$;"? ";
: INPUT H1: PRINT H1
1390 PRINT '"NUMBER OF ";V$;"? "
;: INPUT V1: PRINT V1
1400 PRINT '"ARE THESE CORRECT?"
: INPUT Q$: IF Q$="N" THEN CLS :
 GO TO 1380
1410 IF G(H1)<>-999 THEN PRINT '
"THAT POSITION IS ALREADY
 OCCUPIED BY THE VALUE ";G(H1);"
."'"DO YOU WISH TO REPLACE IT? (
Y/N)": INPUT Q$: IF Q$="N" THEN
CLS : GO TO 1350
```

```
1420 LET G(H1)=V1: INPUT "ANOTHE
R VALUE?";Q$: IF Q$="Y" THEN CLS
 : GO TO 1350
1430 RETURN
```

This module accepts the data which will be used to draw the graph itself.

Commentary

Line 1410. When the array G was set up it was filled with the value -999 to indicate vacant elements, since 0 is unlikely to be used frequently. If an item is input for a position which is not still filled with -999, the user is informed that data has already been input for that position.

Line 1420. The data is placed into the array G. No attempt is made to check that it does fall within the limits specified for the graph, though the user was invited to confirm the data item in line 1400. Note that since the units on the horizontal axis are assumed to proceed in units of 1 from a base of 1, the position of an item on the horizontal axis is also its position in G.

Testing Module 5.3.4

The graph cannot be drawn yet but the module should accept data and inform you if you are overwriting data that is already present.

MODULE 5.3.5

```
1530 REM ***************************
1540 REM DRAW GRAPH
1550 REM ***************************
1560 PRINT AT 0,0;V$;" BASE:";BA
SE;"/LIMIT:";LIMIT: FOR I=1 TO L
EN H$: PRINT AT 21-LEN H$+I,31;H
$(I): NEXT I
1570 GO SUB 1450
1580 FOR I=1 TO H: IF G(I)=-999
THEN NEXT I: PRINT AT 10,3;"NO D
ATA.": STOP
1590 PLOT INVERSE 1; OVER 1;11+I
*LH,11+(G(I)-BASE)/VVAL*LV
```

```
1600 FOR J=I TO H: IF GGG(J)=-999
THEN GO TO 1640
1610 FOR K=J+1 TO H
1620 IF G(K)=-999 THEN NEXT K: I
F K>H THEN GO TO 1650
1630 DRAW LH*(K-J),(G(K)-G(J))/V
VAL*LV
1640 NEXT J
1650 INPUT """ENTER"" TO CONTINU
E";Q$: RETURN
```

This module draws the actual graph based on the data supplied by the user.

Commentary
Line 1560. The names of the units for horizontal and vertical axes are printed in appropriate places.

Line 1580. If there is no data present the program informs the user.

Line 1590. This line takes some unravelling at first sight. What it does is to plot an invisible point where the graph should start. 11 + I*LH is the horizontal position corresponding to the first item of data in the array G. G(I)-BASE is the value of an item of data in relation to the start point of the vertical axis. (G(I)-BASE)/VVAL is the number of units this should represent on the vertical axis. (G(I)-BASE)/VVAL*LV is the height in pixels of the point determined.

Lines 1600-1640. Two loops are needed, one to record the position of the last point plotted, the other to find the next position to be drawn to. There is no requirement that every data space be filled by the user, so the module will skip empty elements in G. Once an item of data has been found, line 1630 draws a line to a point corresponding horizontally to the position of the data in G, taking account of any empty spaces on the way, and vertically to the number of pixels above or below the previous value plotted. (G(K)-G(J)))/VVAL*LV is directly parallel to the expression explained in line 1590.

Testing Module 5.3.5
If you have input any sensible data you should now be in a position to draw a graph. If this is accomplished satisfactorily the program is ready for use.

Summary
It is unlikely that many Spectrum users will want to use a program like this one every day. But it is an example of the kind of tool which can be valuably added to a program library in the knowledge that one day you will want to draw a graph,

but not badly enough to write a special program. You may also have noted, in entering the program, that even though it is fairly bare the addition of small touches like highlighting marks on the axes, the display of unit names and the starting point of the vertical axis can make the difference between a graph that is merely correct and one that is comprehensible and correct. After all, what is the point of storing something if the next time you come to look at it you cannot quite remember what it is meant to represent or what the units are?

Going Further

1) One fairly simple project is to adapt the program so that it will also draw bar charts. The bars could be of variable thickness from application to application so that the only change to the program would be to the module which draws the graph. Having established the value at a particular position, the module would have to draw LH lines down to the horizontal base, or perhaps LH-1 so that a separation is marked between the bars.

2) The program could usefully have a facility to print out the graph without stopping the program to enter COPY in direct mode.

5.4 Renumber

Having suggested that most Spectrum owners would hardly be using the last program every day, I will go to the opposite extreme for this program and assert that you will probably use it more than any other in your library. For those who are unfamiliar with the idea, a renumber program is one that changes the irregular line numbers that develop as most programs are written, to the regular structure seen in most of the programs in this book.

This is not as difficult a task as it might sound. Line numbers are stored at the beginning of each line in two bytes — in the same way as we have stored values in two characters in strings. All that needs to be done is to find the position of the line number that starts the program, POKE into the two positions the line number you want to start with, then move on through the line numbers POKEing numbers which increase by regular intervals. You can do it in three or four lines.

The problem is that renumbering does not stop there because of the small matter of GOTOs and GOSUBs. Scattered throughout the program will be references to the original line numbers. If those line numbers were changed there would be chaos. So we need to renumber GOTOs and GOSUBs that match the changed line numbers.

This is not easy. The way GOTO and GOSUB destinations are recorded is considerably different and more complex than the way line numbers are stored. We have noted before that numeric values normally require five bytes of the Spectrum's memory to allow for the vast range of numbers the Spectrum can accurately express. Unfortunately, in some respects, GOTO and GOSUB destinations employ this more complex form of storage, even though the 9,999 possible line numbers only really require 2 characters to record.

In some ways this does increase the flexibility of the machine — since the destination is regarded as a real number it can be expressed in all the ways the Spectrum will recognise a number. For instance, 1000 + X, 2*A/Y, VAL '2500' would all be valid destinations provided that their results are in the range 1-9999. There are some clever programming tricks in Sinclair Basic which depend upon this capability. When it comes to renumbering, however, the five byte representation is a nuisance. It is made worse by the fact that the destination number, like any real number displayed in a program line, is actually recorded twice in the line, once as a set of characters for you to see and a second time in the five byte form.

The conclusion of all this is that not only do we have to renumber the line, we also have to know if there are any GOTOs or GOSUBs pointing at the line that is being renumbered. If there are we have to change two more numbers by different methods.

Within certain limits that is exactly what this little program will do and, while it is by no means as fast and convenient as a good machine-code program to achieve the same result, MERGEd with your own programs it will do an adequate job until you get round to buying an expensive commercial program or writing your own.

```
9958 STOP
9959 LET T$="": LET X=23635
9960 DEF FN A(X)=PEEK X+256*PEEK
 (X+1)
9961 DEF FN B(S)=256*PEEK S+PEEK
 (S+1)
9962 LET S=FN A(X)
9963 LET LINE=FN B(S): IF LINE>=
9958 THEN GO TO 9976
9964 LET LENGTH=FN A(S+2)
9965 IF PEEK (S+4)=234 THEN GO T
O 9969
9966 FOR I=S+4 TO S+LENGTH+2
9967 IF PEEK I=236 OR PEEK I=237
 THEN GO SUB 9971
9968 NEXT I
9969 LET S=S+LENGTH+4
9970 GO TO 9963
9971 IF PEEK (I+5)=14 THEN GO TO
 9974
```

```
9972 PRINT "NON-STANDARD COMMAND
, LINE ";LINE
9973 STOP
9974 LET T$=T$+STR$ I+CHR$ PEEK
(I+1)+CHR$ PEEK (I+2)+CHR$ PEEK
(I+3)+CHR$ PEEK (I+4)
9975 RETURN
9976 LET BASE=1000: LET X=23635
9977 LET S=FN A(X)
9978 LET LINE=FN B(S): IF LINE>=
9958 THEN STOP
9979 LET LENGTH=FN A(S+2)
9980 FOR I=1 TO LEN T$ STEP 9
9981 IF VAL T$(I+5 TO I+8)=LINE
THEN GO SUB 9990
9982 NEXT I
9983 POKE S,INT (BASE/256)
9984 POKE S+1,BASE-256*INT (BASE
/256)
9985 LET BASE=BASE+10
9986 LET S=S+LENGTH+4
9987 GO TO 9978
9990 FOR J=1 TO 4
9991 POKE (VAL T$(I TO I+4)+J),C
ODE (STR$ BASE)(J)
9992 NEXT J
9993 LET BYTE1=128+INT (LN BASE/
LN 2+1)
9994 LET BYTE2=BASE*65536/(2^(BY
TE1-128))
9995 LET MEMORY=VAL T$(I TO I+4)
9996 POKE MEMORY+6,BYTE1
9997 POKE MEMORY+7,INT (BYTE2/25
6)-128
9998 POKE MEMORY+8,BYTE2-256*INT
 (BYTE2/256)
9999 RETURN
```

The program is not written in modules since the aim is to cram as much as possible into as few line numbers as possible. When you understand the method you may well wish to shorten the program by the use of multi-statement lines.

Commentary
Line 9958. This line ensures that normal execution of the main part of the program being renumbered never reaches the renumber routine.

Line 9959. T$ will be used to record each occurrence of a GOTO or GOSUB in the program together with its location in the Spectrum's memory. X is the address in the Spectrum's memory of the 'system variable' PROG, that is two bytes which record the start address in the memory of the current Basic program.

Line 9960. This function should be recognisable as the start address of the current Basic program. Note that when it is working for its own purposes the Spectrum stores two byte numbers 'back to front' — the least significant of the two bytes comes first.

Line 9961. Just to confuse you, line numbers, which are also two bytes, are stored the right way round. This function will translate two byte line number representation into a more recognisable form.

Line 9962. S is set equal to the address of the start of the program.

Line 9963. LINE is set equal to the actual line number found at this point. When the routine has worked through the program to the point where the renumber routine itself is reached, this section of the program is left.

Line 9964. The two bytes after the line number in any line record the length of the line. This value can be used to move easily on to the beginning of the following line.

Line 9965. Lines beginning with REM (CHR$234) are not examined for GOTOs and GOSUBs. This means that if you have a calculated GOTO like 1000*X, which the program cannot cope with, you can simply put a temporary REM at the beginning of the line and it will cause no problems.

Lines 9966-9968. The line is examined byte for byte for the characters representing GOTO and GOSUB (codes 236 and 237 respectively).

Lines 9969-9970. If nothing is found in the line, the routine moves on to the start of the next line.

Lines 9971-9973. If execution has reached this point it is because a character with a code of 236 or 237 has been found in the line. These lines check that it is a normal GOTO or GOSUB that the routine can deal with. This is done on the basis that every destination will be visibly represented when you look at the line by four digits e.g. GOTO 1000, GOTO 0001. If that is true then the fifth character after the GOTO will be 14 which indicates to the Spectrum that a five byte number follows (the second of the two representations of the destination). If this is not the case the routine stops. On rare occasions the routine will encounter bytes containing 236 or 237 which have nothing to do with a GOTO or a GOSUB and will stop. Having identified the problem, the only solution is to put a temporary REM at the beginning of the offending line.

Lines 9974-9975. If the routine discovers a standard GOTO or GOSUB it stores the address in T$, together with the four bytes which make up the destination.

Line 9976. By the time the routine reaches this point it has run through the program once, recording the position of every GOTO and GOSUB and the lines they point to. The program now sets up a variable BASE which will be used for the first line number.

Lines 9977-9978. The routine starts again at the beginning of the program and begins translating line numbers. Once line 9958 is reached the renumbering will be complete.

Line 9980-9982. Having established the line number the routine scans T$ to see whether it is a line pointed to at any time by a GOTO or a GOSUB. If so, it proceeds to renumber the GOTO or GOSUB in a way explained below.

Lines 9983-9987. The value of BASE is placed into the position occupied by the old line number. BASE is increased by 10 and the routine moves on to the next line number.

Lines 9990-9992. If there is a GOTO or GOSUB to be renumbered, the routine first pokes the characters which make up BASE into the four bytes following GOTO or GOSUB.

Lines 9993-9998. In this section we move on to the manipulation of the complex five byte representation of numbers employed by the Spectrum. This task is simplified by the fact that we are dealing only with positive numbers in the range 1-9999. This means that we only ever have to deal with the first three of the five bytes. There are two basic tasks. The first is to determine the exponent of the renumbered destination when expressed in binary — that is the number of places before the decimal point when the number is written in binary. The first byte of any positive number stored by the Spectrum will consist of 128 plus this exponent and this value is created by line 9993.

The next two bytes record the actual binary representation of the destination. Since we already have the exponent to tell us how many characters there are in this binary number we can store the number with its first '1' in the first of the eight positions in the following byte. Thus if the binary representation were to be 1010101010 this would be stored in the two bytes following the exponent byte as 1010101010000000 and the exponent byte will record the fact that the first 10 digits only are significant. Our final task is to transform the first '1' of our binary number to a zero, indicating to the Spectrum that this is a positive number. The '1' will be reinstated when the number is evaluated.

The necessary number is created by line 9994 without any obvious reference to binary numbers. The exponent and the translated destination are then placed into the first three bytes of the five byte representation. The routine now proceeds with the renumbering of the rest of the program.

Testing 5.4
The first rule to be observed when testing a routine like this one is to record it before you attempt to use it. Programs which poke the Spectrum's memory can go wrong and crash the machine. That does not matter to the Spectrum but you would lose your program. Having saved your renumber routine you will need to give it something to work on; this need only be a three line program such as 1 GOTO 0005, 2 REM, 5 REM. Now change the second statement in line 9963 to IF LINE = 9958 THEN STOP. Run the program, starting at 9959. When the program stops, have T$ printed out. It should look like this: — 237590005.

If this test is satisfactory, correct line 9963 and run the program again from 9959. This time it should actually renumber the lines. Print out BYTE1 and BYTE2. They should be 138 and 65280 respectively. If the program does not work at this stage try inserting some judicious STOP statements at various points to check that the procedure described above is being followed.

Summary
If you can write a routine like this in machine code, go ahead and do so. It will be 100 times faster. But do not get carried away with the idea that fiddling about with things like Sinclair's five byte representation is not possible in Basic. Machine code snobbery can result in some pretty awful programs which do next to nothing, but do it very quickly. So be careful that you really have to leave the comfort of Basic to achieve your aims. Who knows, in 10 years time the only difference between a Basic program and a machine code version may be a thousandth of a second.

Going Further
1) I like my program numbered from 1,000 in 10s; you may not. Why not add a simple mechanism to allow the user to specify the BASE and the spacing between the lines.
2) See how far you can go in shortening the routine by the use of defined functions.
3) The Spectrum can handle GOTOs which point to a non-existent line. This routine will not renumber such GOTOs. Add a function to the program which scans the line numbers to check that there is a destination for each GOTO or GOSUB.

5.5 Unifile II

With Unifile II we return to the theme of the opening chapter of the book, namely the flexible filing of large quantities of information. In the program that follows we see a new application for the methods first discussed in chapter one and we see again the strengths of our modular approach. The numbering of the program is, in the main, that of the original Unifile program and, unlike the other programs in this book, the alterations made have not been renumbered. This is done in order that you may identify exactly where changes and additions have been made to the original program and so that, other than for comments on the actual changes, you may refer to the commentary on the original version.

The new application for which the present program is intended is that of the database. A database, at its simplest, is a collection of information, preferably incorporating ways of adding to the current stock and ways of discovering what is stored there. Unlike the neat and tidy structure of the files created by the original Unifile program, the database needs to be able to accept information whose structure cannot be so easily foreseen. The structure may vary widely from entry to entry. The database is often expected to employ a more sophisticated method of searching, enabling the user to specify a number of characteristics which should be present in the sought-for entry.

This is a fairly tough specification, yet such is the strength of the modular approach to program writing that the present program took something under three hours to write from the original idea to the finished version. In what follows the modules are only commented upon if they differ significantly from the equivalent module in Unifile. In entering the program the reader is advised to first load the original Unifile program and to work by modifying that in accordance with the listing for the current program.

MODULE 5.5.1

```
1000 PAPER 7: CLS : BORDER 7: IN
K 6: PAPER 0: PRINT PAPER 2;"
     UNIFILE                   "
1010 PRINT '"FUNCTIONS AVAILABLE
:"
1020 PRINT '"      1)SET UP NEW F
ILE"
1030 PRINT '"      2)ENTER INFORM
ATION"
1040 PRINT '"      3)SEARCH/DISPL
AY/CHANGE"
1045 PRINT '"      4)TYPE NAMES"
1050 PRINT '"      5)STOP"
```

```
1060 PRINT ''"PLEASE ENTER WHICH
 YOU REQUIRE."
1070 INPUT Z$
1080 CLS
1090 IF Z$="1" THEN GO SUB 1210
1100 IF Z$="2" THEN GO SUB 1440
1110 IF Z$="3" THEN GO SUB 2180
1115 IF Z$="4" THEN GO SUB 3400
1120 IF Z$="5" THEN GO SUB 1150
1130 CLS
1140 GO TO 1000
1150 PRINT AT 10,5; INK 7; PAPER
 2;"FILING SYSTEM CLOSED"
1160 BEEP 2,2
1180 INPUT "Have you input new i
nformation  you wish to save? (Y
/N)";Q$: IF Q$="N" THEN STOP
1190 SAVE "UNIFILE": PRINT '"Rew
ind tape, then press any key to
VERIFY": PAUSE 0: VERIFY "UNIFIL
E": STOP
```

The module is modified at lines 1045 and 1115 to take account of a new function, which will be explained below.

MODULE 5.5.2

```
1200 REM ************************
1210 REM INITIALISE
1220 REM ************************
1230 DIM A$(50,10)
1350 DIM B$(28000)
1360 LET B$(1 TO 4)=CHR$ 2+CHR$
0+CHR$ 2+CHR$ 255
1370 DEF FN A()=256*CODE Y$(2*S-
1)+CODE Y$(2*S)
1380 DEF FN A$()=B$(C TO C+CODE
B$(C)-1)
```

```
1390 LET P=5
1400 LET Y$=CHR$ 0+CHR$ 1+CHR$ 0
+CHR$ 3
1410 LET N=2
1420 RETURN
```

A large proportion of this module has been deleted to take account of the fact that there will be no regular structure of names for the items in each entry. There will, however, be the possibility of attaching names to items and these names will be stored in the array A$.

MODULE 5.5.3

```
2750 REM ************************
2760 REM FUNCTIONAL SUBROUTINES
2770 REM ************************
2780 INPUT Q$
2785 IF LEN Q$>1 THEN RANDOMIZE
: IF Q$(LEN Q$-1)="#" THEN LET Q
$=Q$( TO LEN Q$-1)+CHR$ (VAL Q$(
LEN Q$))
2787 IF LEN Q$>2 THEN RANDOMIZE
: IF Q$(LEN Q$-2)="#" THEN LET Q
$=Q$( TO LEN Q$-2)+CHR$ (VAL Q$(
LEN Q$-1 TO ))
2790 LET Q$=CHR$ (LEN Q$+1)+Q$
2800 RETURN
2810 PRINT A$(I,2 TO CODE A$(I,1
));":";
2820 RETURN
2850 IF FN A$()(2 TO )="*" THEN
RETURN
2860 IF FN A$()(LEN FN A$()-1)="
#" THEN PRINT A$(CODE FN A$()(LE
N FN A$()));":";
2870 PRINT FN A$()(2 TO LEN FN A
$()-2*(FN A$()(LEN FN A$()-1)="#
"))
```

```
2880 LET C=C+CODE B$(C)
2890 GO TO 2850
```

The small routine at line 2780 is altered so that it can recognise label numbers preceded by # and translate the following number into a single character of that code. The routine at line 2850 is changed so that it will print out items until detecting the "*" terminator. The appropriate labels are printed by line 2860 if the # is present.

MODULE 5.5.4

```
1430 REM ************************
1440 REM NORMAL INPUT
1450 REM ************************
1460 LET R$=""
1470 PRINT PAPER 2;"             EN
TRIES                "
1480 PRINT '"COMMANDS AVAILABLE:
"
1490 PRINT '">ENTER ITEM SPECIFI
ED"''">""ZZZ"" TO QUIT"
1500 PRINT "********************
************"
1510 PRINT "FILE SIZE:";P-1;"/";
LEN B$
1540 GO SUB 2780
1550 IF Q$(LEN Q$-1)="#" THEN PR
INT A$(CODE Q$(LEN Q$));":";
1580 PRINT Q$(2 TO LEN Q$-2*(Q$(
LEN Q$-1)="#"))
1590 IF LEN Q$>=4 THEN RANDOMIZE
 : IF Q$(2 TO 4)="ZZZ" THEN RETU
RN
1600 LET R$=R$+Q$
1610 IF Q$(2)<>"*" THEN GO TO 15
20
1620 CLS
```

```
1630 GO SUB 1660
1640 GO TO 1440
```

Rather than requesting a specified number of items, this module now accepts items until it comes across an item which consists of "*", which it takes to indicate the end of the entry. Lines 1550 and 1580 refer to the method of labelling the item. To do this the user adds # followed by a number in the range 1-50 to the end of the item. This is taken to indicate the number of an item in the array A$ and the relevant line of A$ is displayed by line 1550 if the # is detected. Line 1580 ensures that the number is not printed.

MODULE 5.5.5

```
1650 REM ************************
1660 REM PLACE DATA IN FILE
1670 REM ************************
1680 IF P+LEN R$-1<LEN B$ THEN G
O TO 1730
1690 PRINT AT 14,10;"FILE NOW FU
LL"
1700 PRINT ''"    Press any key t
o continue"
1710 PAUSE 0
1720 RETURN
1730 LET POWER=INT (LN (N-1)/LN
2)
1740 LET S=2^POWER
1750 LET T$=R$(2 TO CODE R$(1))
1760 FOR K=POWER-1 TO 0 STEP -1
1770 LET C=FN A()
1780 LET U$=FN A$()(2 TO )
1790 LET S=S+(2^K)*(T$>U$)-(2^K)
*(T$<U$)
1810 IF S>N-1 THEN LET S=N-1
1820 IF S<2 THEN LET S=2
1830 NEXT K
1840 LET C=FN A()
1850 LET U$=FN A$()(2 TO )
1860 IF T$<U$ THEN LET S=S-1
1870 LET B$(P TO P+LEN R$-1)=R$
```

```
1880 LET N=N+1
1890 LET Y$=Y$(1 TO 2*S)+CHR$ IN
T (P/256)+CHR$ (P-256*INT (P/256
))+Y$(2*(S+1)-1 TO )
1900 LET P=P+LEN R$
1910 RETURN
```

No change is made here.

MODULE 5.5.6

```
2170 REM ***********************
2180 REM SEARCH
2190 REM ***********************
2200 LET S=2
2210 PRINT PAPER 2;"
SEARCH                    "
2220 PRINT "COMMANDS AVAILABLE:"
2230 PRINT ">INPUT ITEM FOR NORM
AL SEARCH"'">PRECEDE WITH ""SSS"
" FOR"'" SPECIAL SEARCH"'">PRECE
DE WITH ""III"" TO SEARCH"'" FOR
 FIRST CHARACTER OF ENTRY"'">""E
NTER"" FOR FIRST ITEM ON FILE"
2235 PRINT ">""MMMM"" FOR MULTIP
LE SEARCH"
2240 PRINT "********************
***********"
2250 PRINT "INPUT SEARCH ITEM:";
2260 GO SUB 2780
2270 PRINT Q$(2 TO )
2280 LET S$=Q$
2290 IF LEN S$=1 THEN GO TO 2510
2300 LET C=FN A()
2310 IF LEN S$<5 THEN GO TO 2430
2311 IF S$(2 TO 4)<>"MMM" THEN G
O TO 2320
2312 PRINT "NUMBER OF SEARCH ITE
MS? ";: INPUT SEARCH: PRINT SEAR
CH: DIM M$(SEARCH,10): FOR K=1 T
O SEARCH: PRINT "SEARCH ITEM ";K
;": ";: GO SUB 2780: PRINT Q$(2
TO ): LET M$(K)=Q$: NEXT K
```

```
2313 LET S1=S
2314 FOR K=1 TO SEARCH: LET S$="
MMMM"+M$(K,2 TO CODE M$(K,1)): G
O SUB 2940: IF C4=0 THEN RETURN
2316 IF S=S1 THEN NEXT K: GO TO
2510
2318 GO TO 2313
2320 IF S$(2 TO 4)<>"III" THEN G
O TO 2390
2330 FOR I=S TO N
2340 LET S=I
2350 LET C=FN A()
2360 IF B$(C+1)=S$(5) THEN GO TO
 2510
2370 NEXT I
2380 RETURN
2390 IF S$(2 TO 4)<>"SSS" THEN G
O TO 2430
2400 GO SUB 2920
2410 IF C4=1 THEN GO TO 2510
2420 RETURN
2430 IF FN A$()=S$ THEN GO TO 25
10
2450 IF FN A$()=CHR$ 2+CHR$ 255
THEN RETURN
2460 LET C=C+CODE B$(C)
2470 IF B$(C-1)<>"*" THEN GO TO
2430
2480 LET S=S+1
2490 LET C=FN A()
2500 GO TO 2430
2510 LET C=FN A()
2520 LET C4=0
2530 IF FN A$()=CHR$ 2+CHR$ 255
THEN RETURN
2540 CLS
2550 PRINT "ENTRY ";S-1;":-"
2560 GO SUB 2850
2570 LET S=S+1
2580 PRINT AT 16,0; PAPER 2;"
      SEARCH                   "
```

```
2590 PRINT "COMMANDS AVAILABLE:"
2600 PRINT ">""ENTER"" TO DISPLA
Y NEXT ITEM"'">""ZZZ"" TO QUIT F
UNCTION"'">""AAA"" TO AMEND"'">"
"CCC"" TO CONTINUE SEARCH"
2610 INPUT P$
2620 CLS
2625 IF LEN S$>=4 THEN RANDOMIZE
 : IF P$="CCC" AND S$(2 TO 4)="M
MM" THEN GO TO 2313
2630 IF P$="CCC" THEN GO TO 2300
2640 IF P$="" THEN GO TO 2510
2650 IF P$<>"AAA" THEN GO TO 271
0
2660 LET C=FN A()
2670 CLS
2680 GO SUB 1930
2710 IF P$="ZZZ" THEN RETURN
2720 IF P$="AAA" THEN RETURN
2730 CLS
2740 GO TO 2260
```

Between line 2311 and 2318 a small routine is added to this module which accepts a number of search items and then calls the special search module for each item in succession. If all of the specified character combinations are found within any single entry, that entry is then displayed. Note also the small change to the menu at 2235 and to the continuation command at 2625.

Testing Module 5.5.6

You should now be able to display items, though you cannot use the special search nor the multiple search. If you specify label numbers on input, the item should always be displayed inset 10 characters and preceded by a ':'.

MODULE 5.5.7

```
2910 REM ************************
2920 REM SPECIAL SEARCH
2930 REM ************************
2940 LET C4=0
2950 FOR H=S TO N-1
2960 LET S=H
2970 LET C=FN A()
```

```
2980 LET C1=C
3000 LET C1=C1+CODE B$(C1)
3010 IF B$(C1-1)<>"*" THEN GO TO
 3000
3020 FOR J=C+1 TO C1-LEN S$+5
3030 IF B$(J TO J+LEN S$-5)<>S$(
5 TO ) THEN GO TO 3060
3040 LET C4=1
3050 RETURN
3060 NEXT J
3070 NEXT H
3080 LET C4=0
3090 RETURN
```

A small change is made to this module to take account of the lack of a regular structure to the entry.

Testing Module 5.5.7

You should now be able to conduct searches for character combinations — item preceded by SSS. You should also be able to enter the multiple search mode.

MODULE 5.5.8

```
1920 REM ***********************
1930 REM CHANGE ENTRY
1940 REM ***********************
1950 LET S=S-1
1960 LET C=FN A( )
1970 LET R$=""
1980 PRINT "ENTRY ";S-1;":-"
2000 IF FN A$( )(2)="*" THEN LET
R$=R$+CHR$ 2+"*": GO SUB 3130: G
O SUB 1660: RETURN
2010 PRINT FN A$( )(2 TO LEN FN A
$( )-1);
2015 IF FN A$( )(LEN FN A$( )-1)="
#" THEN PRINT CODE (FN A$( )(LEN
FN A$( )))
```

```
2017 IF FN A$()(LEN FN A$()-1)<>
"#" THEN PRINT FN A$()(LEN FN A$
())
2020 PRINT AT 16,0; PAPER 2;"
         AMEND                 "
2030 PRINT "COMMANDS AVAILABLE:"
2040 PRINT ">""ENTER"" LEAVES IT
EM UNCHANGED"'">""ZZZ"" DELETES
WHOLE ENTRY"'">CHANGED ITEM"'">N
EW ITEM ENDING WITH ""*"""
2050 GO SUB 2780
2060 IF LEN Q$=1 OR Q$(LEN Q$)="
*" THEN LET R$=R$+FN A$()
2070 LET C=C+CODE B$(C)
2080 CLS
2090 IF LEN Q$=1 THEN GO TO 2000
2100 IF Q$(2 TO )="ZZZ" THEN GO
SUB 3130: RETURN
2105 IF Q$(LEN Q$)="*" THEN LET
Q$=Q$(2 TO LEN Q$-1): GO SUB 278
5
2110 LET R$=R$+Q$
2120 GO TO 2000
2130 GO SUB 3130
2140 IF Q$(2 TO )="ZZZ" THEN RET
URN
2150 GO SUB 1660
2160 RETURN
```

Lines 2015 and 2017 reflect the need to translate a label number, if present, from the character of the relevant code to an actual number. If there is no label number the last two characters of the item are printed. The menu and subsequent lines are modified to take account of items with a "*" terminator — when one of these is entered it is stored in the entry, following the item currently on display at the top of the screen. This means that a new item cannot be inserted at the beginning of an entry.

MODULE 5.5.9

```
3100 REM ************************
3110 REM TELESCOPE FILE
```

```
3120 REM ***********************
3130 LET C=FN A( )
3140 LET SHIFT=1000
3150 LET C1=C
3160 LET C3=C
3180 LET C1=C1+CODE B$(C1)
3190 IF B$(C1-1)<>"*" THEN GO TO
 3180
3200 LET C2=C1-C
3210 FOR I=C1 TO LEN B$-1 STEP S
HIFT
3220 IF LEN B$-I+1<SHIFT THEN LE
T SHIFT=LEN B$-I+1
3230 LET S$=B$(I TO I+SHIFT-1)
3240 LET B$(C TO C+SHIFT-1)=S$
3250 LET C=C+SHIFT
3260 NEXT I
3270 LET Y$=Y$(1 TO 2*(S-1))+Y$(
2*(S+1)-1 TO )
3280 FOR I=1 TO N-1
3290 LET S=I
3300 LET C=FN A( )
3310 IF C<=C3 THEN GO TO 3350
3320 LET C=C-C2
3330 LET Y$(2*I-1)=CHR$ INT (C/2
56)
3340 LET Y$(2*I)=CHR$ (C-256*INT
 (C/256))
3350 NEXT I
3360 LET P=P-C2
3370 LET N=N-1
3380 RETURN
```

Changes are made at line 3190 and by deleting line 3170.

Testing Module 5.5.9

The amend function should now be fully operative, allowing deletions, alterations and insertions.

MODULE 5.5.10

```
3400 REM ************************
3410 REM ITEM TYPES
3420 REM ************************
3430 FOR I=1 TO 50 STEP 10
3440 CLS : FOR J=I TO I+9
3450 PRINT J;")";A$(J)
3460 NEXT J
3470 PRINT '''"COMMANDS:"
3480 PRINT '">ZZZ=QUIT"
3490 PRINT ">III=ITEM"
3495 PRINT ">NNN=NEXT PAGE"
3500 INPUT Q$: IF Q$="ZZZ" THEN
RETURN
3505 IF Q$="NNN" THEN CLS : NEXT
 I: RETURN
3510 IF Q$="III" THEN INPUT "NUM
BER? ";TYPE: INPUT "TYPE NAME? "
;Q$: LET A$(TYPE)=Q$: CLS : GO T
O 3440
3520 GO TO 3500
```

This short module allows the user to input labels for items at specified positions in the array A$. There is no specific provision for deletion which can nevertheless be simply accomplished by specifying the relevant line and entering an empty string as its new contents.

Testing Module 5.5.10

If you have previously specified label numbers for some of the items you should now be able to provide some content for the labels and see the labels displayed before the relevant items by the display module.

Summary
It would be foolish to suggest that a program like this one is as useful as a fast machine code database, capable of conducting a complex search in seconds. Nevertheless the program works and has superior capabilities to some cheap database programs which have been sold for personal microcomputers. The multiple search is a time-consuming luxury that you will not want to use very often on a large file. You may, because of specific needs of your own, come to use this version of Unifile more frequently than the original.

The real lesson to be drawn is that a major new application has been rendered simple by the modular approach which allowed us to clearly identify the areas which needed modification.

Going Further
1) Having warned against machine code snobbery it has to be admitted that with an application like this one we are at the frontiers of what can be usefully accomplished in Basic on a machine with the speed of the Spectrum. My own ZX81 versions of Unifile incorporate short machine code routines to accomplish the time-consuming searches. If database applications are going to be crucial to your use of the Spectrum then that is the direction in which you will have to go.

5.6 Typist
Not every useful program has to be hundreds of lines long. This one will give you a big push on the way to touch-typing if you use it properly. It is short because, as with the geography tutor we looked at earlier, it is left to the user to input and delete the material the program will work on, in the form of DATA statements. Hence there are no lengthy modules for accepting the input of data and deleting items of data. The program is a reminder of the constant need to examine what you intend to do with your Spectrum and ask the question; does it have to be that sophisticated? Sometimes the answer is clearly yes, as in the case of the true general purpose program. Very often it is clear that the structure of a program is such that it is very unlikely to be of any use for anything other than the single purpose for which it was designed.

MODULE 5.6.1

```
1270 REM ***********************
1280 REM USR CHARACTERS
1290 REM ***********************
1300 RESTORE : FOR I=0 TO 63: RE
AD BYTE: POKE USR "A"+I,BYTE: NE
XT I: RETURN
1310 DATA 0,0,0,0,0,7,4,4
1320 DATA 0,0,0,0,0,255,0,0
1330 DATA 0,0,0,0,0,224,32,32
1340 DATA 4,4,4,4,4,4,4,4
```

```
1350 DATA 32,32,32,32,32,32,32,3
2
1360 DATA 4,4,7,0,0,0,0,0
1370 DATA 0,0,255,0,0,0,0,0
1380 DATA 32,32,224,0,0,0,0,0
1390 RETURN
```

This module fills the first eight characters of the user-defined graphics area with the characters necessary to draw a small square around a letter. These squares will be used to represent typewriter keys on the screen. The method used is similar to that employed in the game Tracker.

MODULE 5.6.2

```
1000 REM ***********************
1010 REM PRINT KEYBOARD
1020 REM ***********************
1030 INK 0: PAPER 6: CLS : DIM O
$(32): GO SUB 1270
1040 CLS : PRINT "ABCABCABCABCAB
CABCABCABCABCABC  D ED ED ED ED
ED ED ED ED ED E  FGHFGHFGHFGHFG
HFGHFGHFGHFGHFGH"
1050 PRINT " ABCABCABCABCABCABCA
BCABCABCABC  D ED ED ED ED ED ED
 ED ED ED E  FGHFGHFGHFGHFGHFGHF
GHFGHFGHFGH"
1060 PRINT "  ABCABCABCABCABCABC
ABCABCABCABC  D ED ED ED ED ED E
D ED ED ED E  FGHFGHFGHFGHFGHFGH
FGHFGHFGHFGH"
1070 PRINT " ABCABCABCABCABCABCA
BCABCABCABC  D ED ED ED ED ED ED
 ED ED ED E  FGHFGHFGHFGHFGHFGHF
GHFGHFGHFGH"
1080 PRINT OVER 1;AT 1,0;" 1  2
 3  4  5  6  7  8  9  0"
```

```
1090 PRINT OVER 1;AT 4,0;"   Q   W
  E   R   T   Y   U   I   O   P"
1100 PRINT OVER 1;AT 7,0;"    A
S   D   F   G   H   J   K   L   E"
1110 PRINT OVER 1;AT 10,0;"  C
Z   X   C   V   B   N   M   S"
```

This module draws a rough copy of a typewriter keyboard in the top half of the screen, using the characters defined by the previous module.

Commentary
Lines 1040-1070. These strings of letters are entered in the graphics mode and will, in fact, create the square outlines of the keys.

Lines 1080-1110. Each key is labelled with the main letter or number if contains. The space key is left blank and the CAPS SHIFT, SYMBOL SHIFT and ENTER keys are labelled with their inverse initials.

Testing Module 5.6.2
Put a temporary STOP at the end of the module and you should be able to print out a recognisable keyboard on the screen.

MODULE 5.6.3

```
1400 REM ************************
1410 REM DATA FOR TESTS
1420 REM ************************
1430 DATA "THIS IS A SPECTRUM TY
PING TEST"
1440 DATA "JUST TYPE WHAT YOU SE
E"
1450 DATA "DONT LOOK AT THE KEYB
OARD"
1460 DATA "STOP"
```

This module will be used to contain the data for typing tests. Individual strings should not be longer than 32 characters. The module must be terminated with a

DATA line containing STOP which is used as a signal to reset the DATA pointer in the next module.

MODULE 5.6.4

```
1120 REM ************************
1130 REM ACCEPT INPUT
1140 REM ************************
1150 LET TOTAL=0: LET RIGHT=0
1160 READ A$: IF A$="STOP" THEN
RESTORE 1430: READ A$
1170 PRINT INK 1;AT 16,0;O$;AT 1
6,0;A$'O$: PRINT AT 17,0;
1180 FOR I=1 TO LEN A$
1190 LET T$=INKEY$: IF T$<>"" TH
EN GO TO 1210
1200 GO TO 1190
1210 LET TOTAL=TOTAL+1: BEEP .1,
30: IF T$<>A$(I) THEN PRINT PAPE
R 5;T$;CHR$ 8;: GO TO 1190
1220 LET RIGHT=RIGHT+1
1230 PRINT BRIGHT 1;T$;
1240 NEXT I: PRINT AT 21,25;INT
(RIGHT/TOTAL*100);"%  "
1250 INPUT "MORE? (Y/N) ";Q$: IF
 Q$<>"N" THEN GO TO 1160
1260 STOP
```

This module prints out a string to be typed and invites the user to copy it, on the screen, without referring to the actual keyboard. Incorrect keystrokes are not accepted but a record is kept of the error rate and this is displayed at the end of each string.

Commentary
Line 1160. This line cycles through the data in module 3 and restores to the beginning of the DATA if STOP is encountered.

Lines 1180-1240. This loop accepts the actual input — the loop variable is only incremented for correct keystrokes.

Line 1210. Incorrect keystrokes are displayed for the user to see, distinguished by a cyan background. Note the use of the control character, CHR$ 8, to move the print position back one when the incorrect character has been displayed, so that the print position stays in the same place when an incorrect character is entered.

Lines 1230. Correct keystrokes add to the string being typed. The BRIGHT characteristic is set in order that the user may be sure that spaces have been entered.

Testing Module 5.6.4
If you have entered some data in Module 3, you should now be able to run the program and see the keyboard displayed. The first string in the data area should be displayed under it and you should be able to enter an attempt to retype it.

Summary
The usefulness of this program depends on whether or not you are prepared to take it seriously. Used with a decent typing tutor from the library to provide the right kind of exercises it can be a very effective tool. To begin with you will probably find it easier to stick to capital letters, or lower case, without mixing them with punctuation or symbols. When you are ready the program will deal with mixed characters plus the symbols with SYMBOL SHIFT.

Going Further
1) Using the method outlined on page 131 of the Spectrum manual add a timing function to the input, then alter the program so that it will print out a series of strings amounting to, say, 1,000 characters. Take the time when you begin to input and when the test is completed and you will have, when taken together with the percentage of keystrokes, a good indicator of your progress.
2) Alter the display so that it only shows the keyboard when you make a mistake — perhaps more than one mistake on the same character — and removes it when the character has been correctly entered.

CHAPTER 6

AND FINALLY SOME FUN — Home thoughts for the Spectrum
You will, perhaps already have gathered from the overall form of this book that I do not consider games the be-all and end-all of home computing. My suspicion is that games are a fall-back for those who have discovered the fascination of computing but not yet explored the ways in which the power of the micro can enhance their daily living. Nevertheless, games have their place, depending, of course, on the game. Putting an uninteresting game on to a micro does not make it any better and user-defined characters do not change the fact that, in Basic, the Spectrum is too slow to play Invaders type games with any real degree of satisfaction.

Micros excel at games which require thought. In what follows you will find two games which depend on thought rather than speed of reactions. The first of them, Missile, looks at first sight a straight copy of the alien-zap type of game but requires some real calculation on the part of the player. Next comes Tracker, an infuriating game where you hunt an invisible quarry. Finally, I have included a simple sort routine which should prove useful for addicts of word puzzles and other games which have to use string or numeric sort.

6.1 Missile

You cannot win this game. In the end the ravening alien hordes will swoop down the screen and get you;your job is to take as many of them with you as you can. Your weapons consist of missiles capable of carrying warheads of varying strength, fired from six missile bases. The alien ships, represented by numbers in the range 0-9, descend randomly, one line at a time from the top of the screen. If they reach the bottom of the screen, their strength is deducted from your stock of warheads. On each turn the player is invited to specify the base from which he will fire, the angle at which the missile will travel — from directly upwards to 45 degrees to the right, the height at which the missile will explode — provided the missile does not hit anything first, and the power of the warhead — input as a power of two up to a maximum of 4 — i.e. 16.

When the missile explodes, if it has actually hit an alien ship it will wipe twice its own value off the power of that ship. An alien ship bordering the square in which the missile explodes will be reduced in strength by the equivalent of the missile's power. Ships with a space of one square between them and the missile will lose strength equivalent to half the missile's power, and so on. If an alien ship is reduced in strength below zero it disappears. More aliens are generated on each move.

Every five moves a supply ship, represented by a "*", starts a descent from the top of the screen amongst the alien ships. If it succeeds in landing it will increase your stock of warheads by 100. But if at any point it should become caught up in the circle of destruction created by a missile it will be lost. The score consists of the total amount of damage which the player inflicts on the alien ships and the game concludes when the stock of warheads is exhausted. One final complication is that the player has a limited amount of time in which to make any input; varying levels of difficulty can be set for this. If this time is exceeded or an inappropriate input is made, the aliens move down one line unhindered.

MODULE 6.1.1

```
1000 REM ***********************
1010 REM VARIABLES
1020 REM ***********************
1030 DIM A$(608): DIM C$(4,6): D
IM C(4): DIM D(4,2): DIM O$(32)
1040 LET C$(1)="BASE?": LET C$(2
)="ANGLE?": LET C$(3)="DELAY?":
LET C$(4)="POWER"
1050 LET U$="": LET SCORE=0: LET
 W=100: LET S=1: LET G=1
1060 LET D(1,1)=49: LET D(1,2)=5
4: LET D(2,1)=48: LET D(2,2)=57:
 LET D(3,1)=48: LET D(3,2)=57: L
ET D(4,1)=48: LET D(4,2)=54
1070 BORDER 0: PRINT INK 2; PAPE
R 6;AT 10,8;"MISSILE ATTACK"
1080 INPUT "Please input desired
 difficulty level (0-10):";H: LE
T H=500-45*H
```

The use of these variables will be explained in the course of the program. The module also accepts the difficulty level.

MODULE 6.1.2

```
1910 REM ************************
1920 REM GENERATE ALIENS
1930 REM ************************
1940 LET G=G+1: FOR I=1 TO INT (
RND*(G/5)+1)
1950 LET A=(RND*30+1)
1960 LET SH=INT (RND*10)
1970 LET A$(A)=CHR$ (48+SH)
1980 NEXT I
1990 IF INT ((G-5)/10)=(G-5)/10
THEN LET A$(A)="*"
2000 PRINT AT 0,0;A$: RETURN
```

This module generates the alien ships.

Commentary
Line 1940. The number of aliens generated increases with the number of turns so far.

Line 1950. The position of an alien ship.

Lines 1960-1970. A character between 0 and 9 is generated.

Line 1990. Every fifth move a supply ship is generated.

Line 2000. The array which holds the game board is printed.

Testing Module 6.1.2
Calling this module up should result in random numbers being printed at the top of the screen.

MODULE 6.1.3

```
2010 REM ***********************
2020 REM MOVE SCREEN
2030 REM ***********************
2040 LET A$(33 TO 608)=A$(1 TO 5
76): LET A$(1 TO 32)=O$: PRINT A
T 0,0;A$
```

The game board is shifted down the screen one line.

Testing Module 6.1.3
Calling up this module after the last should result in the random numbers moving down the screen.

MODULE 6.1.4

```
1790 REM ***********************
1800 REM MISSILE TRACK
1810 REM ***********************
1820 LET M=577+5*(C(1)-1)
1830 FOR I=1 TO 18
1840 IF A$(INT M)<>" " THEN RETU
RN
1850 LET A$(INT M)="+"
1860 PRINT AT 0,0;A$
1870 IF I=C(3) THEN RETURN
1880 LET A$(INT M)=" "
1890 LET M=M-32+SIN C(2)
1900 NEXT I: RETURN
```

This module moves a '+' representing the player's missile up the screen.

Commentary
Line 1820. The square above the base is specified.

Lines 1830-1900. Provided there is no obstacle and that the specified maximum height has not been obtained, the missile is moved 32 spaces up the single-dimension array and then back a number of spaces to represent the angle at which the missile travels. The net effect is that the missile moves up and to the right.

Testing Module 6.1.4

If you input a number, in radians, for the missile's angle (C(2)), and maximum height (C(3)), and a base number (C(1)), then call this module, you should see the missile move up the screen.

MODULE 6.1.5

```
1450 REM ************************
1460 REM COMMAND CYCLE
1470 REM ************************
1480 INK 0: PRINT AT 20,0;O$;O$
1490 PRINT AT 21,0;"SCORE:";SCOR
E;,"WARHEADS:";W;"   "
1500 PRINT AT 20,0;
1510 FOR I=1 TO 4
1520 PRINT C$(I);
1530 FOR J=1 TO H+10
1540 LET T$=INKEY$: IF T$<>"" TH
EN GO TO 1570
1550 NEXT J
1560 PRINT AT 10,5;"DEFAULT ON "
;C$(I)
1565 FOR H=1 TO 200: NEXT H: LET
 U$="": GO SUB 2010: GO SUB 1910
: GO TO 1480
1570 BEEP .1,20: IF U$<>"" OR I<
>3 THEN GO TO 1600
1580 IF CODE T$>57 OR CODE T$<48
 THEN GO TO 1560
1590 LET U$=T$: PAUSE 25: GO TO
1530
1600 IF U$="" THEN GO TO 1630
1610 IF CODE T$>57 OR CODE T$<48
 THEN GO TO 1560
1620 LET T$=U$+T$: LET U$=""
1630 IF CODE T$>57 OR CODE T$<48
```

```
 THEN GO TO 1560
1640 IF CODE T$<D(I,1) OR CODE T
$>D(I,2) THEN GO TO 1560
1650 LET C(I)=VAL T$
1660 PRINT C(I);"_" AND I<>4;
1670 NEXT I
1680 LET I=I-1
1690 LET C(2)=C(2)*PI/36
1700 LET C(4)=2^C(4)
1710 IF C(4)>W OR C(4)>16 THEN G
O TO 1560
1720 LET W=W-C(4)
1730 IF W>0 THEN GO TO 1770
1740 PRINT AT 10,3;"YOU ARE OUT
OF WARHEADS."
1750 PRINT AT 11,6;"YOUR SCORE W
AS ";SCORE
1760 STOP
1770 PRINT AT 21,0;"SCORE:";SCOR
E,"WARHEADS:";W;"   "
1780 RETURN
```

This module accepts the player's commands and defaults if the correct times are not kept.

Commentary

Lines 1510-1565. The four commands, whose names are stored in C$, are printed and then the loop at 1530 gives the player a short period in which to press a key. If no key is pressed the program defaults and the aliens move down.

Lines 1570-1670. Depending upon which command is being input, the module tests that a key pushed falls within limits that are stored in the array D. If the limits for any command are exceeded, the module defaults.

Line 1690. The angle input is multiplied by five, expressed in radians.

Lines 1710. An upper limit of 16 is set on the power of a missile since for higher values it is possible that invalid characters may be generated at certain points during the program.

Testing Module 6.1.5
You should now be able to input the four commands within the limits laid down in the array D — line 1060. The program should default if the limits are exceeded or if there is no input.

MODULE 6.1.6

```
1180 REM ************************
1190 REM LETHALITY
1200 REM ************************
1210 PRINT AT 20,0;O$;O$
1220 PRINT AT 20,5;"*CALCULATING
 LETHALITY*"
1230 LET M1=INT (M/32)
1240 LET M2=INT (M-32*M1)
1250 LET R=INT (.5+LN C(4)/LN 2)
1260 FOR J=M1-R TO M1+R
1270 PRINT BRIGHT 8;AT 0,0;A$
1280 PRINT BRIGHT 1;AT M1,M2-1;A
$(INT M)
1290 FOR K=M2-R TO M2+R
1300 IF 32*J+K<1 OR 32*J+K>608 T
HEN GO TO 1400
1310 IF J>=0 AND J<=21 AND K>0 A
ND K<33 THEN PRINT BRIGHT 1; OVE
R 1;AT J,K-1;" "
1320 IF A$(32*J+K)="+" THEN GO T
O 1400
1330 IF A$(32*J+K)=" " THEN GO T
O 1400
1340 LET D=ABS (K-M2)
1350 IF ABS (J-M1)>ABS (K-M2) TH
EN LET D=ABS (J-M1)
1360 LET E=INT (C(4)/(2^(D-1)))
1370 LET A$(32*J+K)=CHR$ (CODE A
$(32*J+K)-E)
1380 IF CODE A$(32*J+K)<48 THEN
LET SCORE=SCORE+CODE A$(32*J+K)-
48: LET A$(32*J+K)=" "
1390 LET SCORE=SCORE+E
1400 NEXT K
1410 NEXT J
```

```
1420 IF A$(INT M)="+" THEN LET A
$(INT M)=" "
1430 INK 0: PAPER 5: PRINT AT 0,
0;A$
1440 RETURN
```

This module calculates the effect of an explosion on the alien ships.

Commentary

Lines 1230-1240. The co-ordinates of the missile are expressed in 2-dimensional terms.

Line 1250. R is the range of the circle of destruction created by the explosion.

Lines 1260-1410. With these loops, character positions within a range of R of the missile's explosion point are examined. If the position under examination is empty or contains the missile itself, no action is taken. If the position contains one of the alien ships, its value is decremented according to the power of the missile and its distance from the alien ship. If the ship's value has been reduced to less than 0, the ship is removed.

Testing Module 6.1.6

Calling this module after Module 4 should result in a highlighted square being printed on the screen at the last position of the missile, the size of the square being dependent on the power of the missile.

MODULE 6.1.7

```
2050 REM ***********************
2060 REM PENALTIES AND BONUSES
2070 REM ***********************
2080 IF A$(577 TO 608)=O$ THEN R
ETURN
2090 FOR I=0 TO 31
2100 IF A$(577+I)="*" THEN LET W
=W+100
2110 IF CODE A$(577+I)>42 THEN L
ET W=W-CODE A$(577+I)+48
2120 NEXT I
```

```
2130 LET A$(577 TO 608)=O$: PRIN
T AT 18,0;O$
2140 PRINT AT 0,0;O$
2150 IF W>0 THEN RETURN
2160 PRINT AT 10,3;"ALIEN ATTACK
 PRESSED HOME."
2170 PRINT AT 11,9;"YOU ARE DEAD
."
2180 PRINT AT 12,7;"YOUR SCORE W
AS ";SCORE
2190 STOP
```

In the event of alien shops reaching the bottom of the screen, this module subtracts their value from the player's stock of warheads.

MODULE 6.1.8

```
1090 REM ************************
1100 REM MAIN LOOP
1110 REM ************************
1120 PRINT AT 19,0;"1####2#####3#
###4#####5#####6#######"
1130 GO SUB 1910
1140 INK 0: PAPER 5: PRINT AT 0,
0;A$
1150 PRINT AT 20,0;O$;O$
1170 GO SUB 1470: GO SUB 1820: G
O SUB 1180: GO SUB 2010: GO SUB
1910: GO TO 1150
```

This module prints the bases at the bottom of the screen and then calls up the various subroutines in sequence.

Testing Module 6.1.8
You should now be able to play the game.

Summary
This is not a fast game but it is worth the trouble of entering it for the simple reason that it is extremely addictive. Played at the higher levels of difficulty the player is under constant pressure to make decisions and at every level a respectable score (1500 and above) requires quick thinking and some accurate calculation.

The program also provides an example of the way a single dimensional array can be used to store a whole-screen game and manipulate it with ease. The method of giving a timed input at lines 1530-1550 will be found useful in a variety of games where it is desirable to put the player under some pressure.

Going Further
1) This is a program which simply cries out to be ornamented with some user-defined graphics. Characters could be defined for the missile and for the various alien ships. In that case the lines at 1370 and 1380 will need to be altered so that the characters proceed from a base of CODE 144 rather than 48.

6.2 Tracker
This is an infuriating game which will have you doubting your sanity or the proper functioning of your Spectrum. It is a game played on a 30 by 18 board, one of the squares on which hides your invisible quarry. It is your task to track down the quarry but each time you make a guess the quarry makes a secret move. Your only advantages are that the quarry's move is always the same within any one game and that you have a special indicator which shows the direction of the quarry every time you make a guess at its position. Full instructions are printed in the game itself.

As to tactics, it is wise to treat the two components of the quarry's move — vertical and horizontal — as separate and try to identify one before being distracted by the other. You need to be very careful that you have actually determined the correct direction in which the quarry is travelling. It is all too easy to work on the assumption that the quarry is moving across the board from left to right — on the basis of two or three guesses and the accompanying clue — when all the while it was moving in the opposite direction.

MODULE 6.2.1

```
2180 REM ***********************
2190 REM USR CHARACTERS
2200 REM ***********************
2210 RESTORE : FOR I=1 TO 8: FOR
 J=0 TO 7: READ B: POKE USR CHR$
 (143+I)+J,B: NEXT J: NEXT I: RE
```

```
TURN
2220 DATA BIN 00000000,BIN 01111
000,BIN 01100000,BIN 01010000,BI
N 01001000,BIN 00000100,BIN 0000
0010,BIN 00000001
2230 DATA BIN 00001000,BIN 00011
100,BIN 00101010,BIN 01001001,BI
N 00001000,BIN 00001000,BIN 0000
1000,BIN 00001000
2240 DATA BIN 00000000,BIN 00011
110,BIN 00000110,BIN 00001010,BI
N 00010010,BIN 00100010,BIN 0100
0000,BIN 10000000
2250 DATA BIN 00010000,BIN 00100
000,BIN 01000000,BIN 1111111,BI
N 01000000,BIN 00100000,BIN 0001
0000,BIN 00000000
2260 DATA BIN 00001000,BIN 00000
100,BIN 00000010,BIN 1111111,BI
N 00000010,BIN 00000100,BIN 0000
1000,BIN 00000000
2270 DATA BIN 00000001,BIN 00000
010,BIN 00000100,BIN 01001000,BI
N 01010000,BIN 01100000,BIN 0111
1000,BIN 00000000
2280 DATA BIN 00001000,BIN 00001
000,BIN 00001000,BIN 00001000,BI
N 01001001,BIN 00101010,BIN 0001
1100,BIN 00001000
2290 DATA BIN 10000000,BIN 01000
000,BIN 00100000,BIN 00010010,BI
N 00001010,BIN 00000110,BIN 0000
1111,BIN 00000000
```

This module loads the first 8 user-defined characters with 9 arrows which will be used to indicate the direction of the quarry.

Testing Module 6.2.1

Running this module should result in the spaces A-H in the user-defined area being filled with the arrows.

MODULE 6.2.2

```
1900 REM ************************
1910 REM INSTRUCTIONS
1920 REM ************************
1930 PRINT INK 3;AT 0,11;"INSTRU
CTIONS"
1940 PRINT "This is a hunting ga
me."'"The hunting ground is an
18 by"'"30 board."'"The quarry
is invisible."
1950 PRINT '"Each turn the quarr
y makes a"'"secret move. This mo
ve does not"'"change during a pa
rticular hunt."
1960 PRINT '"The move can be up
to six spaces"'"up or down and s
ix spaces left"'"or right."
1970 PRINT '"Press any key for m
ore"'"instructions.": PAUSE 0: C
LS
1980 PRINT '''"Each turn consist
s of:"
1990 PRINT '"1) An invitation to
 input your"'"estimate of the po
sition of the"'"quarry."
2000 PRINT '"2) An arrow will ap
pear in your"'"specified square,
indicating the"'"direction of th
e quarry."
2010 PRINT '"3) The quarry will
move."
2020 PRINT '"Press any key to co
ntinue.": PAUSE 0: CLS
2030 PRINT ''"At the start of ea
ch turn you"'"have the opportuni
ty to review"'"the hunt so far."
2040 PRINT '"This is done by ent
ering 0 when"'"the DOWN co-ordin
ate is called"'"for."
2050 PRINT '"You can start the r
```

```
eview at any"'"previous move but
 you are"'"limited to reviewing
20 moves"'"in any one hunt."
2060 PRINT '"These 20 reviews ma
y be taken"'"all at once or in b
atches."
2070 PRINT '"Any key to start.":
 PAUSE 0: RETURN
```

A full set of instructions to the game. Whether or not you include them in this game or in other games you design, depends on who is going to play.

MODULE 6.2.3

```
2080 REM ************************
2090 REM SET DIFFICULTY
2100 REM ************************
2110 CLS
2120 PRINT '''"There is a diffic
ulty factor"'"built into the gam
e."
2130 PRINT '"This consists of an
 entirely"'"random move every so
 often."
2140 PRINT '"The difficulty fact
or ranges"'"from 0 to 10."
2150 PRINT '"0 means no random m
ove at all."
2160 INPUT INK 6;"Please input y
our desired"'"difficulty factor:
",E
2170 LET E=(11-E)*2+2+100*(E=0):
 CLS : RETURN
```

This module sets a difficulty factor. In the event that zero is input, the random move is made only after 100 moves — by which time the game is over.

MODULE 6.2.4

```
1000 GO SUB 2190: BORDER 0: INK
1: PAPER 7: PRINT AT 10,12;"TRAC
KER"
1010 INPUT "Do you want instructi
ons? (Y/N)"'Q$: CLS : IF Q$="Y"
OR Q$="y" THEN GO SUB 1910
1020 GO SUB 2080
1030 REM ************************
1040 REM VARIABLES
1050 REM ************************
1060 LET A=0: LET C=20: LET C1=0
: LET T=0: DIM M(100,4): DIM O$(
32)
1070 LET R1=6-INT (RND*13)
1080 LET R2=6-INT (RND*13)
1090 LET P1=INT (RND*18+1)
1100 LET P2=INT (RND*30+1)
```

This module presents the option of instructions and sets up the various arrays on which the program is based.

MODULE 6.2.5

```
1110 REM ************************
1120 REM INITIAL BOARD
1130 REM ************************
1140 CLS : LET A$="1234567890123
4567890123456789O": PRINT " ";A$
1150 FOR I=1 TO 18: PRINT A$(I):
 NEXT I: GO SUB 1370
```

This module prints out a framework of numbers around the board as a guide to the user.

MODULE 6.2.6

```
1370 REM ***********************
1380 REM PRINT BOARD AND MOVE
1390 REM ***********************
1400 PAPER 5: INK 1
1410 FOR I=1 TO 9: PRINT AT I*2-
1,1;" _ _ _ _ _ _ _ _ _ _ _ _ _
_ _"
1420 PRINT AT I*2,1;"_ _ _ _ _ _
 _ _ _ _ _ _ _ _ _ _": NEXT I
1430 INK 1: PAPER 7
1440 PRINT AT 19,0;O$;O$;O$
1450 IF T=0 THEN RETURN
1460 PRINT AT M1,M2;CHR$ (143+D)
1470 IF A<>1 THEN RETURN
1480 IF T/E=INT (T/E) THEN PRINT
 AT 21,0;"RANDOM MOVE FOLLOWED"
1490 RETURN
```

This module prints out the board on which the game will be played. It also prints the relevant user-defined arrow for a particular move and informs the user if a random move is about to be made.

Testing Module 6.2.6

Although many of the variables have not yet been defined, if a temporary STOP is installed at line 1160, you should be able to RUN the program, inspect the instructions, specify a level of difficulty and see the board and its surrounding grid printed on the screen.

MODULE 6.2.7

```
1160 REM ***********************
1170 REM INPUT AND DIRECTIONS
1180 REM ***********************
1190 INK 0: LET T=T+1: IF T>100
THEN CLS : PRINT AT 10,0;"SORRY-
CAN'T TAKE ANY MORE MOVES.": STO
P
```

```
1200 LET O$=""
1210 PRINT AT 19,23;"MOVE ";T
1220 PRINT AT 21,17;"(0 FOR REVI
EW)"
1230 PRINT AT 19,1;"DOWN:";: INP
UT M1: PRINT M1
1240 IF M1>18 OR M1<0 THEN PRINT
 ">OUT OF RANGE": PRINT AT 19,0;
O$: GO TO 1210
1250: PRINT AT 20,0;O$: IF M1=0
THEN GO SUB 1660: GO TO 1210
1260 PRINT AT 21,0;O$;AT 20,1;"A
CROSS:";: INPUT M2: PRINT M2
1270 IF M2>30 OR M2<1 THEN PRINT
 ">OUT OF RANGE";AT 20,0;O$: GO
TO 1260
1280 PRINT AT 21,0;O$
1290 LET M(T,1)=M1: LET M(T,2)=M
2
1300 IF M1=P1 AND M2=P2 THEN GO
TO 1600
1310 LET M3=(M1<P1)-(M1>P1)+1
1320 LET M4=(M2<P2)-(M2>P2)+2
1330 LET D=M3*3+M4
1340 IF D>4 THEN LET D=D-1
1350 LET M(T,3)=D
1360 GO SUB 1370: GO SUB 1530: G
O TO 1190
```

This module accepts the user's guess as to the position of the quarry and records it for later review. The appropriate user-defined arrow to indicate the direction of the true position is calculated.

Commentary
Line 1290. The player's moves are stored in the array M.

Lines 1310-1350. These lines translate the direction of the quarry, represented by P1 and P2, into the appropriate arrow. This too is stored in the array M at a place corresponding to the current move.

Testing Module 6.2.7

You should now be able to define a guess as to the position of the quarry and an arrow should appear pointing roughly in the correct direction — which can be checked by reference to P1 and P2. The program should not accept moves which fall outside the limits of the board.

MODULE 6.2.8

```
1500 REM ************************
1510 REM MOVE INCREMENT
1520 REM ************************
1530 LET P1=P1+R1: LET P2=P2+R2
1540 IF T/E<>INT (T/E) THEN GO T
O 1570
1550 LET P1=INT (P1+RND*6+1): LE
T P2=INT (P1+RND*6+1)
1560 PRINT AT 21,0;"RANDOM MOVE"
1570 LET P1=P1+18*(P1<1)-18*(P1>
18)
1580 LET P2=P2+30*(P2<1)-30*(P2>
30)
1590 RETURN
```

This module make the quarry's move, including a random move where necessary.

Commentary

Line 1530. P1 and P2 are the co-ordinates of the quarry. R1 and R2 are the random move elements which are added to P1 and P2 on each move, being set in the variables section.

Line 1540. The variable E is set according to the level of difficulty. Every E moves the random move is made, increasing the difficulty.

Lines 1570-1580. These two lines ensure that, if the quarry moves off the board in any direction it reappears on the other side of the board — a wrap-around effect.

Testing Module 6.2.8

You should now be able to input a series of moves.

MODULE 6.2.9

```
1600 REM ************************
1610 REM SUCCESS AT LAST
1620 REM ************************
1630 PRINT AT 10,13;"GOT IT"
1640 INPUT "Another game? (Y/N)"
,Q$: IF Q$="Y" THEN GO TO 1030
1650 STOP
```

This module announces the player's success when, or if, the quarry is found.

Testing Module 6.2.9
Rather than wait to track down the quarry, RUN the game and, when your guess is requested, STOP the program, print out P1 and P2 in direct mode. Start the program again with GOTO 1190 and input the correct co-ordinates, which should call up this module.

MODULE 6.2.10

```
1660 REM ************************
1670 REM REVIEW OF GAME
1680 REM ************************
1690 LET A=1: PRINT AT 19,0;O$;O
$;O$
1700 IF C1>=C THEN GO TO 1780
1710 PRINT AT 6,13;"REVIEW"
1720 PRINT AT 8,4;"REVIEW ALLOWA
NCE ";C;" MOVES"
1730 PRINT AT 10,8;"YOU HAVE USE
D ";C1
1740 PRINT AT 19,1;"LAST MOVE WA
S No.:";T-1
1750 PRINT AT 21,1;"INPUT FIRST
No. FOR REVIEW:";: INPUT T1: PRI
NT T1
1760 FOR J=T1 TO T-1
1770 LET C1=C1+1
1780 IF C1>C THEN PRINT AT 10,4;
```

```
"REVIEW RIGHTS EXHAUSTED": PAUSE
 200: GO TO 1860
1790 LET M1=M(J,1): LET M2=M(J,2
): LET D=M(J,3)
1800 GO SUB 1370
1810 PRINT AT 19,6;"REVIEW OF MO
VE:";J
1820 PRINT AT 21,20;"(0 TO QUIT)
"
1830 INPUT Q$: PRINT AT 19,0;O$;
O$;O$
1840 IF Q$="0" THEN GO TO 1860
1850 NEXT J
1860 LET T=T-1
1870 LET M1=M(T,1): LET M2=M(T,2
): LET D=M(T,3)
1880 GO SUB 1370
1890 LET A=0: RETURN
```

You may have wondered why each move and the arrow corresponding to it are stored in the array M. This module uses the data stored in M to reconstruct previous moves and the clues given for re-examination.

Testing Module 6.2.10

You should now be able to call up a review of previous moves by inputting zero when asked for the down co-ordinate. If this module is satisfactory, the program is ready for use.

Summary

This game is a classic example of dressing-up. The game started as a tiny thing which fitted into the memory of a 1K ZX81. It was fun to play so the board was expanded to make it more of a challenge. Then, because it had become very difficult, the review function was added. Finally, the random move completed the process. The moral is that it is always well worth playing around with simple ideas, even it they appear far too trivial, for with a little bit of disguise you could have the successor to Space Invaders on your hands.

Going Further

1) One definite improvement would be an end-of-game facility which allowed moves to be reviewed, together with the position of the quarry on each turn.

6.3 Word sort

If you like wordgames, and do not mind waiting a couple of hours, you will need a string sort routine. It is an efficient sorting method capable of cutting down on the time taken putting items in order.

MODULE 6.3.1

```
1460 REM ************************
1470 REM SORT
1480 REM ************************
1500 LET A=INT (LN N/LN 2): LET
F=2^A-1
1510 LET F=INT (F/2): IF F=0 THE
N RETURN
1520 LET D=N-F: LET B=1
1530 LET A=B
1540 LET E=A+F: IF A$(A)<A$(E) T
HEN GO TO 1570
1550 LET B=B+1: IF B>D THEN GO T
O 1510
1560 GO TO 1530
1570 LET T$=A$(A): LET A$(A)=A$(
E): LET A$(E)=T$
1580 LET A=A-F: IF A<1 THEN GO T
O 1550
1590 GO TO 1540
```

This module bears the closest study. Up to now we have used a variety of methods to avoid sorting material, preferring to find the correct place for one item at a time. That place is stored in a pointer array rather than the main array being put into the correct order. When a large number of small items are to be input this can be a cumbersome procedure, with a tedious wait after each entry, while the correct place is found. In these circumstances it is far better to input data in whatever order it comes to hand and to sort it after all the items have been entered.

Many programs use a sort and many of the sorts used in home brewed programs are stupendously inefficient. This is not merely a fine point of style; an inefficient sort in a quite simple program can easily be the lengthiest process, requiring a tiresome period of waiting whenever new items of data are input. One program intended for the Spectrum's predecessor, the ZX81, published in a prominent magazine, took 20 minutes to sort 100 items of data into alphabetical order. The method used in this module reduced that time to three minutes.

The sort employed is known as the Shell-Metzner. It works by scanning the data to be sorted and comparing pairs which may be swapped if they are in the wrong order. To begin with, the distance between the items of each pair is the largest power of two which is less than the total number of items of data. The sort starts at one and compares the item of data at that position with, say, the item at position 64 in the case of 100 items of data. The data is scanned until there are no further possible pairs this distance apart. The gap is then reduced and the comparison of pairs begins again at the beginning.

One of the best ways to understand the sorting method in detail is to write the numbers 1 to 20 on slips of paper then, with a notebook handy to record the variables, perform the sort on the basis of the module, just as if you were the Spectrum. When you have finished you may still find it difficult to see quite why it worked, but it does and it is one of the most efficient sorts available.

Commentary
Lines 1500-1510. These two lines find the largest power of two which is less than the total number of items to be sorted — in fact less one.

Line 1520. D is a marker; if the current gap between the items of pairs is F, then the first item of the last possible pair will be at N-F. B records the first item of the current pair.

Line 1540. A$ is dimensioned with N items. Note that items are actually being sorted into reverse length order in the module.

Line 1570. This line performs the actual swap if line 1540 has found the items in the pair to be in incorrect order.

Line 1580. In the event that an item has been swapped backwards, say from item 82 to item 50, the scan moves back to examine the pair of which it is now the second item i.e. 18/50.

Testing Module 6.3.1
You will not be able to test this routine until you develop a program which needs to use a sort. The program can easily be changed to sort numeric rather than string data, by dimensioning a variable A with N items.

POSTWORD

If you have worked through all the programs in this book, apart from deserving a medal of some kind, you are now the proud possessor of a library of programs. True, it is not the biggest library in the history of computing, but it contains the tools to tackle a wide variety of tasks if only you will adapt the programs to your own specific needs. More than that, it is an indication, a hint — no more — of what your Spectrum is waiting to achieve for you.

The programs in this book are ideas that worked for me, that interested me, that solved problems that I had. Because they are mine some of them will miss the mark when you come to apply them yourself and to your own problems. In that case change them, mutilate them, break them up for spares. They will be much better when you have made them your own.

INDEX

The numbers after the index entries refer to the relevant module numbers.

Other titles by the same author

The Working Spectrum is the first volume of a series of practical computer books by David Lawrence.

The Working Dragon 32 will be published in 1983

David Lawrence is also a regular contributor to *Popular Computing Weekly,* Britain's only weekly home computer newspaper and magazine.